WOMEN IN EUROPEAN HISTORY AND CULTURE

VOLUME II

Women In Medieval/Renaissance Europe

by
SUSAN HILL GROSS & MARJORIE WALL BINGHAM

WOMEN IN WORLD AREA STUDIES

ESEA Title IVC WWAS
St. Louis Park and Robbinsdale Schools

© Copyright 1983

Glenhurst Publications, Inc.

Publishers of Women's History Curriculum
Central Community Center/6300 Walker St./St. Louis Park, MN 55416 (612) 925-3632

Picture Credits

Roman Ruins — Photo: Margo Sprague

Queen Isabella I of Spain — Bradley Smith

Queen Elizabeth I of England — Colonial Williamsburg Foundation

Queen Margaret of Navarre — Musee Conde, Chantilly. Giraudon photograph

Medieval Gate Tower — Photo: Margo Sprague

'August' from "Tres Riches Heures du Duc de Berry" — Musee Conde, Chantilly. Giraudon photograph

The Nuns' Kitchen at the Abbey of Fontrevault, France — Photo: Margo Sprague

Nunnery Officials. Page from a Manuscript of 'La Sainte Abbaye' — The British Library, London

Nuns in Choir. Miniature of Poor Clares from the 'Psalter of Henry VI' — The British Library

St. Catherine of Siena — Die Fresken des Antoniazzo Romano by Adolf Gottschewski

Sketch of Joan of Arc, by Clement de Fauquembergue — Archives Nationales, Paris. Photograph by Gjon Mili

Vision of St. Teresa, Bernini — Alinari/Art Resource, Inc.

Katherine von Bora from Cranach — Women of the Reformation in Germany and Italy by Roland H. Bainton. By permission of Augsburg Publishing Company

Jeanne d'Albret — Musee Conde, Chantilly. Giraudon photography

Peasant Women and Men Harvesting — Rheinisches Landesmuseum Bonn

Wife and Husband Bankers — Reunion des Musees Nationaux. Louvre Museum

Women Working at Farm Labor (Detail of a miniature from the "Tres Riches heures du Duc de Berry") — Musee Conde, Chantilly

Midwife Attending Childbearing Woman — Wellcome Institute Library, London

Medieval Family Gathers Together for Supper ("January") — The Pierpont Morgan Library, New York

The Seder — Hebrew Union College Library — Jewish Institute of Religion. Cincinnati Haggadah (Ms 444)

Woman in Cloak and Veil — Foto Stadtarchiv Worms

From *Witchcraft in Europe 1100-1700,* Alan C. Kors and Edward Peters, editors. Copyright ©1972 by the University of Pennsylvania Press. By permission of the publisher:

Women as Witches Bring a Hailstorm

A Woman Being Seduced by the Devil

The Dismemberment and Burning of a Child-Victim

The Hanging of the Chelmsford Witches

Swimming a Witch

Balthasar Bekker

Portrait of Charlotte of France by Jean Clouet. Bequest of John R. Van Derlip in memory of Ethel Morrison Van Derlip. Reproduced by permission of The Minneapolis Institute of Arts

The Lady Giving Orders in her Kitchen — Mansell Collection

Nun and Monk Tilting — The Beinecke Rare Book and Manuscript Library, Yale University

Christine de Pisan presents a Book to a Patron — The British Library, London

Book of Hours "Virgin Reading While Joseph Rocks the Babe" — The Walters Art Gallery, Baltimore

Artemisia Gentileschi: "Judith" — Alinari/Art Resource, Inc.

Artemisia Gentileschi: Self-portrait as 'La Pittura' — The Royal Collection, Lord Chamberlain's Office

The Nun Hroswitha Presenting one of her Books to Otto the Great — The Complete Woodcuts of Albrecht Durer, Dr. Willi Kurth, editor

A Well-Born Lady's Pursuits: Love and Sport — Mansell Collection

Garlanding an Illicit Lover (Courtly Love Tradition) — Mansell Collection

Madonna and Child — The Book of Kells. "Trinity College Library" Dublin

The Golden Madonna — Bildarchiv Foto Marburg

Spanish Madonna and Child — Museu d'Art de Catalynya, Barcelona

Flight into Egypt, Gislebertus — Cathedral of Autun, France

Virgin and Child, School of Auvergne, France — The Metropolitan Museum of Art, New York. Gift of J. Pierpont Morgan 1916

Virgin and Child on a Curved Throne, Byzantine School — National Gallery of Art, Washington, D.C., Andrew W. Mellon Collection 1937

Virgin and Child, Notre Dame, Paris — Alinari/Art Resource, Inc.

Virgin Mary and Jesus — Reunion des Musees Nationaux. Louvre Musee

Madonna and Child, Lorenzo Monaco — Alinari/Art Resource, Inc.

Adoration of the Shepherds, Domenico Ghirlandaio — Alinari/Art Resource, Inc.
The Small Cowper Madonna; Raphael — National Gallery of Art, Washington, D.C. Widener
    Collection 1942
Virgin of the Rocks; Leonardo da Vinci — The National Gallery, London

Medieval/Renaissance Europe
Acknowledgments

Excerpt from *Queen of Navarre: Jeanne d'Albret,* page 381, by Nancy Roelker. Copyright ©
    1968. Reprinted by permission of Harvard University Press.
Excerpt from *European Witch Trials,* pages 24-26, by Richard Kieckhefer. Copyright ©1976.
    Permission by University of California Press.
Excerpt from *MS* magazine, March 1980, page 94, quoted in Judith Thurman, "Lost Women:
    Louise Labe." By permission of *MS* Foundation for Education and Communication, Inc.
Excerpts from *The Woman Troubadours,* pages 81, 89, 159, by Meg Bogin. Copyright ©1976.
    By permission of Paddington Press.
Excerpts from *Catherine of Siena,* pages 58-60, by Sigrid Undset. Copyright ©1954. By
    permission of Sheed and Ward, London, publishers.
Excerpts from *The Life of St. Leoba* by Rudolf, Monk of Fulda, in *The Anglo-Saxon Missionaries
    in Germany,* C.H. Talbot, translator. By permission of Sheed and Ward, publishers.
Excerpts from *Women of the Cell and Cloister,* pages 254, 256, by Ethel Rolt-Wheeler.
    Copyright ©1913. By permission of Methuen London, publisher.
Excerpt from *The Art of Ecstasy: Teresa, Ernini and Crashaw,* page 40, by Robert T. Peterson.
    Reprinted with the permission of Atheneum Publishers.
Excerpt from *Medieval English Nunneries,* pages 134-135, by Eileen Power. By permission of
    Cambridge University Press, publisher.
Excerpts from *Anglo-Saxon Wills,* pages 11-15, 21, 85, 93, by Dorothy Whitelock. By permission
    of Cambridge University Press, publisher.
Excerpts from *Witchcraft in the Middle Ages,* pages 76, 109, 210, by Jeffrey Burton Russell.
    Copyright ©1972. Cornell University Press.
Poem from *Women in English Economic History,* pages 19-20, by F.W. Tickner. Copyright
    ©1923. By permission of J.M. Dent & Sons Ltd, publishers.
Excerpt from *Witchcraft: The Heritage of a Heresy,* page 33, by Hans Sebald. Copyright ©1978
    by Elsevier Science Publishing Co., Inc. Reprinted by permission of Elsevier North Holland,
    Inc., New York.
Excerpts from *Female Scholars: A Tradition of Learned Women Before 1800,* pages 108, 129,
    by Jeanie R. Brink. Copyright ©1980 Eden Press Inc. Reprinted by permission.
Ballad from *The Witchcraft Papers,* pages 73-75, Peter Haining, editor. Copyright ©1974.
    "Peter Haining Collection." By permission of Robert Hale Limited, London.
Excerpt from *Women Healers in Medieval Life and Literature,* page 105, by Murial Joy Hughes.
    Copyright ©1943. By permission of King's Crown Press, Division of Columbia University
    Press.
Excerpts from "Germany and Its Tribes" in *The Complete Works of Tacitus,* pages 713-719,
    Moses Hadas, editor, Alfred John Church and William Jackson Brodribb, translators.
    Copyright ©1942. By permission of Random House, Inc.
Excerpt from *Women in Judaism: The Status of Women in Formative Judaism,* page 102, by
    Leonard Swidler. (Metuchen, N.J.: Scarecrow Press, 1976). Copyright ©1976 by Leonard
    Swidler. Reprinted by permission of Scarecrow Press.
Excerpt from *The Jew in the Medieval World, A Source Book 315-1791,* pages 399-400, by Jacob
    R. Marcus. By permission of American Jewish Archives (The Sinai Press).
Excerpt from *The Trials of the Lancashire Witches: A Study of 17th Century Witchcraft,* pages
    130-131, by Edgar Peel and Pat Southern (Taplinger Publishing Co., Inc., 1970). ©1969 by
    Edgar Peel and Pat Southern. Reprinted by permission.
Excerpts from *Joan of Art in History, Legend and Literature,* pages 10, 12, 14, by Ingvald
    Raknem. Copyright ©1971. By permission of Universitetsforlaget.
Excerpts from *Doctrine for the Lady of the Renaissance,* pages 17-18, 259, by Ruth Kelso.
    Copyright ©1956. By permission of University of Illinois Press.

Excerpt from *The Education of Women During the Renaissance,* page 99, by Mary Agnes Cannon (Washington, D.C.: Catholic University of America, 1916).

Excerpt from *Woman Under Monasticism,* page 327, by Lina Eckenstein (Cambridge: Cambridge University Press, 1896).

Excerpt from "Craftswomen in the Livre des Metiers," *Economic Journal,* 5, 1895, pages 209-228, by E. Dixon.

Excerpt from *Women of Medieval France,* pages 293-295, by Pierce Butler (Philadelphia: Rittenhouse, 1908).

Excerpt from *The Plays of Roswitha,* pages 37-47, Christopher St. John, translator (New York: Benjamin Blom, 1923).

Excerpt from "Women in Norman Ireland," in *Women in Irish Society,* page 18, by Katharine Simms; Margaret MacCurtain and Conncha O'Corrain, editors. Copyright ©1979. Reprinted by permission of Greenwood Press, Inc.

Excerpt from *English Midwives,* page 90-92, by James Hobson Aveling (London: Hugh K. Elliott, 1967) (1872).

Excerpt from *The Memoirs of Gluckel of Hameln,* Marvin Lowenthal, translator. Introduction Copyright ©1977 by Schocken Books Inc. Reprinted by permission of Schocken Books Inc.

Excerpt from *Women in the Middle Ages,* page 33, by Sibylle Harksen (New York: Abner Schram, 1975).

Excerpts from *Witchcraft in Europe 1100-1700,* pages 114-121, 274, 275, Alan C. Kors and Edward Peters, editors. Copyright ©1972. University of Pennsylvania Press, Philadelphia. Reprinted by permission of University of Pennsylvania Press.

Excerpts from *Midwives and Medical Men,* page 3 and 34, by Jean Donnison (New York: Schocken Books, 1977).

Library of Congress Catalog Card Number 83-20787

International Standard Book Numbers
0-914227-02-5 Paper Edition
0-914227-03-3 Library Edition

TABLE OF CONTENTS

Europe in the 14th Century

Introduction

The title *Women in Medieval/Renaissance Europe* reflects the overall thesis of this book. The thesis states that the history of women throughout medieval and Renaissance times cannot be divided in the usual way into two separate time periods. The traditional division of history into two distinct eras—medieval times and the Renaissance—is more applicable to the history of men than that of women.

When the Renaissance is seen from the point of view of men, it has been pictured, as its name suggests, as a rebirth, a watershed between medieval and modern times. Seen in this way, the Renaissance represents the beginning of modern business, science, exploration and nation states. It also pictures an era in which philosophers scorned the immediate past of the Middle Ages and tried instead to recapture and redefine the more distant classical past of ancient Greece and Rome. Renaissance art and literature looked to Greece and Rome for models, as did the new humanist philosophies.

But for women's history there appear to be fewer differences between these two historical time periods. The usual progress made in the Renaissance, of science and the arts, described in traditional histories is not as pronounced for women's history. Some historians have even seen a decline in the personal freedom and power of women in the Renaissance when compared with medieval times.[1] The title of this book is meant, then, to imply this

---

[1]See Ruth Kelso, *Doctrine for the Lady of the Renaissance* (Urbana: University of Illinois Press, 1956) and Joan Kelly-Gadol, 'Did Women Have a Renaissance?' in *Becoming Visible: Women in European History*, Renata Bridenthal and Claudia Koonz, eds (Boston: Houghton Mifflin Co., 1977).

difference in perspective between men's and women's history. The thesis of the book is that there was no great change for women in most areas of human activity between the medieval and Renaissance periods. Also, in some ways, or in some areas of Europe, women's status actually declined and there were fewer roles open to women in the Renaissance than in medieval times. Therefore, the two periods can be seen as one continuous period with various ups and downs for women, depending on time, place and class rather than, as with men's history, two distinct periods.

Women in Medieval/Renaissance Europe covers the period of European history from about the 5th to the mid-17th century. Because of shifting values and the wide variety of customs, this 1200 years of European history is difficult to date and to describe. For women's history, however, this era was united by the central theme of what was seen as the ideal woman. Writings of the Roman Catholic Church emphasized the ideal Christian woman as pious, virtuous and submissive. She was the opposite of the Biblical Eve, seen as temptress and rebel. The ideal of the pious, virtuous and submissive woman dated from Roman times and continued through the Renaissance. This standard of perfection was brought by the Church[2] in their missionary teaching to many diverse ethnic groups such as the Celts, the Saxons and the Franks, as well as to the four main economic classes of the time—royalty, nobility, peasantry and urban worker. But this ideal frequently did not fit the actual roles that women of the time fulfilled as daughters, wives and mothers or even as religious women such as Beguines or nuns.

No historian has as yet written a complete chronological history of women in this time period. One problem has been that the sources of information are in so many different classical languages, such as Latin, Ancient Greek, Old French, Middle German and Old and Middle English. Another problem has been that many sources have been lost, like the poetry of a whole group of women poets of Lyon, France, now known only as the Lyon poets. But sources that give information on medieval/Renaissance women still exist and more are being uncovered. Using computer analysis of birth, marriage, death, manorial and other records, new insights into the condition of women's lives are being formulated. A more complete picture of women of medieval/Renaissance times is beginning to take shape.

The Cultural Universals

The arrangement of *Women in Medieval/Renaissance Europe* views the condition of women in this historical time period through the vehicle of the cultural universals. This model is used instead of the traditional historical divisions of medieval and Renaissance periods. These six areas serve as topics for organizing this long time period. The activities of all human cultures can roughly be divided into six cultural universals. The cultures of all human societies include these six areas of activities. These broad categories can be visualized as a pie.

---

[2]"The Church" in this unit refers to the dominant and unifying force of Western Europe in medieval times—The Roman Catholic Church (see glossary).

Cultural Universals

Cultural Universals

Although all societies have elements of each cultural universal, some put far more emphasis on one or more areas than others...the pieces of the pie may vary in size.

Politics

How does the society decide what the laws should be? Who makes the decisions—an individual or group, queen, king, chief or adult group members? How are these rules enforced, by whom and who can appeal in court? What are the punishments for disobeying these rules?

Religion

What ideas does the group have about spiritual matters? What god or gods are worshipped and how is worship conducted? Is it at home or in a more formal meeting? Who conducts the services or meetings? Are there differences within religious activities depending on the sex of the participants?

Economics

What are the means of survival— how do people acquire food, shelter and other goods that seem important to their physical health and comfort? How are goods distributed among people? Who does the necessary work? How is it divided?

Social Arrangements

Who is considered the most and the least important? Why? Under what conditions do the positions (status) or roles (expected behavior) change? Does age, sex, intelligence, inherited wealth or titles influence arrangements? How are the cycles of life (birth, adulthood, marriage, death) dealt with?

Education

Does the society have a formal educational system that includes schools and agreed-to curriculum, specific subjects and hired teachers? Is the curriculum the same for all classes of both sexes? Are the schools the same? If the schooling is informal—not done by teachers in schools—how are the young people taught the rules of society and its accumulated knowledge? Is it done by parents, through initiation, schools, elder story tellers, religious leaders—or even by one's peers?

Art

How do people in the society express their individual and group values in sculpture, painting, weaving, pottery, music and other art forms? Are they practical and useful, decorative and beautiful or expressive models of deep societal values? What symbolic meanings do their art forms have concerning the particular group?

Since all societies include these six areas of human activity, these categories make a useful model for arranging information about women's history in a particular time period. Each chapter of this book attempts to emphasize one of these

3

cultural universals—although not exclusively so. Women may have had high status in one area of human activity, religion perhaps, but may have had little influence in other areas, such as in art or government. By using this model, it is hoped that a more balanced view of women of various classes and places in these time periods can be achieved.

★ ★ ★ ★ ★ ★

Generally, historians who separated the medieval and Renaissance worlds, stressed a shift in values from the otherworldly, spiritual values of medieval times to the worldly ones of the Renaissance. Again, this seems to have occurred for men but not for women. Women were still expected in Renaissance times (at least by male writers) to be as pious, virtuous and submissive as they had been in medieval times.[3]

If a chronology of women's history were theorized for this long, combined medieval/Renaissance era, it might look something like this:

1-500 A.D.
   The Roman Matron and the Christian Virgin: Upper class married women were seen as ladies, but the Church stressed virginity as an ideal. The strongest misogynist (anti-woman) writing was during this time period.

500-1000 A.D.
   Women as Survivors: Peasant women struggled for survival, working in the fields, noble women acted to protect property, barbarian queens led armies and were frequently rulers. The 7th and 8th centuries were high points for women as designated saints of the church.[4]

1000-1200 A.D.
   Women as Acceptable Civilizers: The courtly love tradition stressed chivalry and a new ideal was the noble woman as inspirer of secular arts and actions. The Virgin Mary was stressed in religion.

1300-1500 A.D.
   Women in Secular Worlds: Convents were enclosed and the secular courts became more influential in educating women. Witchcraft trials were frequent and the accused were mostly women.

1450-1650 A.D.
   Women in the New Humanism: Emphasis was placed on the importance of women being literate. Marriage customs came to view wife and husband in separate but equal spheres. Witchcraft trials reached their height.

The Renaissance saw some changes in attitudes toward women from medieval times. The idea that women as well as men had a right to become literate was especially stressed. But the pious, virtuous and submissive woman remained the ideal. The years from about 400-1650 were often chaotic, violent and at times even comic; women met the events of those times in much the same way as men by using their abilities and wit to survive—and sometimes to prevail.

---

[3]For further reading, Ruth Kelso, *Doctrine for the Lady of Renaissance* (Urbana: University of Illinois Press, 1956).

[4]Tibbetts Schulenburg, ''Sexism and the Celestial Gynaeceum from 500 to 1200,'' Vol. 4, No. 2, *Journal of Medieval History* (June, 1978), p. 122.

Points to Consider

1. Though many changes for women occurred in this era, in general, what was the ideal for women?

2. What addition did the Renaissance give to the definition of a good woman?

Chapter 1
Political Women in
Medieval/Renaissance
Europe

A. The Early Middle Ages
Barbarian Women as Admirable Women

Historians often have called the period in European history from the fall of the Roman Empire (476 A.D.) to about the 10th century, the *Dark Ages.* They have meant that the era is dark in the sense of something unknown and records are scarce. They also meant dark as something bad or evil—an era that was economically impoverished and politically chaotic. Recently, some historians have questioned this view. Research indicates evidence of technological and economic gains after the fall of Rome such as the invention of the heavy, deeper cutting plow which increased food production.[1] Both the spread of Christianity in this period and the growth of the Roman Catholic Church in Western Europe acted as politically unifying forces. In addition, the so-called barbarian tribal peoples who had defeated the Romans produced some truly fine leaders, such as Alfred the Great of England, who governed their various areas of Europe well. Many of these historians say the really chaotic period of famines, plague and lawlessness began in the 3rd century, well before the final collapse of the Roman Empire, and that the Dark Ages were really times of slow economic recovery from this Roman period of decline.

Other evidence suggests that this era should not necessarily be thought of as the *Dark Ages* and that certain of these tribal groups had ideas about the roles for women that were more open than those of the Romans. Although customs varied and some Roman laws were

---

[1]See for example: William Carrol Bark, *Origins of the Medieval World* (NY: Anchor Books, 1960) and Marc J. B. Bury, *History of the Later Roman Empire* (London: Dover Publications, 1958) and the *Invasion of Europe by the Barbarians* (London: Russell and Russell, 1963).

Remains of the Roman Empire can be found in Great Britain, Continental Europe and North Africa.

beneficial to tribal women, still, many of these tribal groups seemed to have expected women to fill positions of power. Women frequently took an active part in government, inherited and controlled property and engaged in war.

These expectations for women were in contrast to the earlier Roman ideal of the matron whose concerns were limited to domestic chores and to her family. They also contrasted with later Christian medieval time, whose ideal woman was pious, virtuous and submissive.[2] By looking at views of the Roman historian Tacitus and the Anglo-Saxon chronicles we can see how these tribal women are portrayed in accounts from Roman and early medieval times.

★ ★ ★ ★ ★ ★

The Roman historian, Tacitus, in the 1st century A.D., observed some of these Northern European/non-Roman women. In an essay called, "Germany and Its Tribes," Tacitus described the society and government of various groups that had already begun to press Rome's borders to the north and would eventually conquer Rome. Tacitus' observations of these people included a description of some of the Germanic customs and laws concerning women. He thought that these tribal peoples had many valuable ideas about women's roles which he admired. The following descriptions are taken from Tacitus' essay and illustrate his ideas of women's roles in some Germanic groups that later conquered Rome.

★ ★ ★ ★ ★ ★

---

[2]Later selections will discuss various views of women in the High Middle Ages.

The Women in German Tribes
Marriage Customs:

"[The tribal] marriage code, however, is strict, and indeed no part of their manners is more praiseworthy...The wife does not bring a [dowry] to the husband, but the husband to the wife. The parents and relatives are present, and pass judgment on the marriage-gifts—not such as a bride would deck herself with, but oxen, a steed, a shield, a lance, and a sword. With these presents the wife is engaged, and she herself in her turn brings her husband a gift of arms. This they count their strongest bond of union,...Lest the woman should think herself to stand apart from aspirations after noble deeds and from the perils of war, she is reminded by the [marriage] ceremony...that she is her husband's partner in toil and danger, destined to suffer and to dare with him alike both in peace and in war. The yoked oxen, the harnessed steed, the gift of arms, proclaim this fact."

Marriage Age:

"...The young men marry late, and their vigor is thus unimpaired. Nor are the maidens hurried into marriage; the same age and a similar stature is required; well-matched and vigorous they wed, and the off-spring reproduce the strength of the parents..."
[Marriage age for Roman women was 13 and these young girls were often married to older men. Tacitus seems to feel that the higher age for women marrying might have helped to prevent problems in child bearing and would lower the birth rate.]

Participation in War and Respect for Women:

"Tradition says that [German] armies already wavering and giving way have been rallied by women who have vividly represented the horrors of captivity, which the Germans fear with such extreme dread on behalf of their women...The strongest tie by which a state can be bound is being required to give, among the number of hostages, maidens of noble birth. They even believe that the female sex has a certain sanctity and ability to foretell the future and they do not despise their [women's] counsels, or make light of their answers..."
[Although some Roman leaders privately accepted women's advice and control, publicly they were excluded from the senate and military leadership.][3]

★ ★ ★ ★ ★ ★

Although laws and customs varied from one area to another, most allowed a wide variety of activities for women. Not only Germanic women enjoyed these privileges but Anglo-Saxon women of England (c. 6th to llth centuries) also occupied many public roles.

---

[3]Alfred John Church and William Jackson Brodribb, trs., "Germany and Its Tribes," *The Complete Works of Tacitus* (NY: Modern Library, 1942), p. 713-719.

For example, the Anglo-Saxon Chronicles before the time of William the Conqueror, (1066 A.D.) mention women such as Hilda, a 7th century abbess who ruled over two double monasteries where both men and women lived as celibates. Judith, step-mother of Alfred the Great, herself a great reader, encouraged Alfred to devote himself to his studies.[4] An example of one woman ruler was Aethelflaed, daughter of Alfred the Great, frequently mentioned in the chronicle called the "Mercian Register."[5] She ruled her area of England for eight years after her husband, Lord Aethelred died. The chronicle casually stated how she took various new territories, built forts, occupied the town of Derby and, finally, how *"the people of York had promised her...that they would be under her rule..."*[6]

What is interesting about the description of these women in the early English chronicles (before the conquest of England by William I)is not that they are mentioned or that there even were such women rather it is that the storytellers treat them so casually and not as exceptional curiosities. Most positions of power were held by men as the system of selecting rulers was patriarchal. Thus, the system favored males, still, these early chroniclers were not at all astonished by females holding power or at their ability to rule effectively.[7]

Historians of the High Middle Ages (11th-15th centuries), treated these early Anglo-Saxon women rulers quite differently from earlier chroniclers. For example, in one 12th century version, Aethelflaed was made the daughter of Aethelred and ruled only because he was old and sick. Apparently this writer could not conceive that a widow could rule alone.[8] Often these female rulers are described in these later histories as being *"manlike"* in their actions, acting *"above the nature of her sex"* or, in one case, using *"woman's tricks"* to rule.[9]

Here, female qualities are treated as negative and undesirable, male as positive and desirable. In these later descriptions, powerful females are considered to be oddities or as mannish women not behaving properly. Later descriptions appear to represent an important change in attitude from the chroniclers of early Anglo-Saxon times who treated the fact of women in power as an unremarkable occurrence.

There is evidence, then, that women occupied positions of power during the Dark Ages. Queens such as Brunhild and Fredegunde achieved fame for their leadership while other women fulfilled a variety of public roles as expected of them.

---

[4]Betty Bandel, "English Chroniclers' Attitude Toward Women", *Journal of the History of Ideas,* Vol. XVI (1955), p. 114-115.

[5]F.T. Wainwright, "Aethelflaed Lady of the Mercians," *The Anglo-Saxons,* Peter Clemoes, ed. (London: Bowers and Bowers, 1959), p.54.

[6]Quoted in Bandel, p. 115.

[7]*Ibid.,* p. 114-115.

[8]*Ibid.,* 116.

[9]*Ibid.,* p. 117-118.

Points to Consider

1. Why do you think the Germanic men gave the women oxen for a bridal gift and the women gave the men weapons? Why does Tacitus approve of these gifts?

2. How does the age of marriage for Germanic girls compare to that of boys? How does this compare to Roman marriage ages?

   Why do you think Tacitus prefers the Germanic custom of later marriage age for girls?

3. What specific things did these Germanic women do in time of war to help their side be victorious?

4. How were powerful and notable women described in the early Anglo-Saxon Chronicles? How did these descriptions change in the later histories?

5. What might these changes in description indicate about a change in the status of women?

   What might have been some other explanations for these changes in Anglo-Saxon histories even though women's roles had not changed?

B. The Queens
Power Behind the Throne and On the Throne

There is one office of king, the ruler, though he may have limited or unlimited power. But there have been four types of queens in European history. These four categories are:

Queen Consort

This title was given to show that a woman was wife of the king and her position depended upon his.
Since kings were expected to marry and produce more kings, the list of queen consorts is long. Their power depended on the influence they had on the king, which, in the case of Margaret of Navarre or the Carolingian, Queen Judith, was considerable.

Queen Regina

This title was given to the woman who directly inherited the throne and ruled by herself. Examples of this sort of queen would be Elizabeth I of England (1533-1603), Isabella of Castile (1451-1504) and Christina of Sweden (1626-1689).[1]

Queen Regent

This was the title given to women who took over the powers of the throne when the king was away or, if the king was still a minor, until he grew up. Her power might vary depending on circumstances but could be considerable, even to that of absolute monarch. The list of women regents is a lengthy one. For example, in French history, Louise of Savoy, Anne of Brittany, Anne of Austria, Blanche of Castile and Catherine de Medici served as powerful regents.

Queen Dowager

This title was used to indicate that a woman had been consort queen,

---

[1] In Christina's case her title was actually defined by the Swedish Parliament as 'King' to show her power; she was therefore legally "King Christina."

but her husband had died. The usual role for dowager queens was to retire from the court and, particularly in early medieval times, to enter a convent. They might return to their dower land instead, which was theirs according to feudal law, and continue rule over these lesser lands. Perhaps the best example of a dowager queen who did not retire from public life was Eleanor of Aquitaine. She had been married to two kings (divorced and then widowed), but held Aquitaine and served her two kingly sons of England, John and Richard the Lion Hearted, who lacked the "patience and realistic practicality"[2] that she had.

The role, then, of queen might differ according to what sort of queen she was—and she might be expected to play several of these four queenly roles within her lifetime. Margaret of Denmark, for example, was married to the king of Norway. At his death, she became regent, or Lady of Norway for her son. She was elected as daughter of the former king to the Danish throne and because of her abilities was also elected to the Swedish throne.[3] Whatever sort of queen, however, she generally had several duties to perform. In the next sections the role of consort queen and reigning queens will be described.

★ ★ ★ ★ ★ ★

A Queen Consort's Role

No one ever sat down to write a job description for a queen. A king's power was also vague, and quarrels, like those between King John of England and his barons which led to the Magna Carta, were frequent between kings and their nobles, kings and the church. But a queen's role—particularly queen consort—was an even more vaguely defined

position. Queens were generally crowned in religious ceremonies either with their husband-kings or later. Though they might, as in French Capetian ceremonies, be consecrated with simple oil rather than specially blessed oil for kings,[4] nevertheless there was a sense that the queen shared something of the king's power. Her life was not private but, like the king's, a public one. Though no job description of a consort queen exists, based on these queens' actual activities a description might include the following:

- She should bring political advantages from her own country or territories to her husband's country.

- She was expected to produce children, particularly sons, to continue the dynasty.

- She often acted as backup ruler if the king were absent in war or unable to rule because of illness.

- She set the tone of the court through her patronage or religious, educational and artistic enterprises.

- She often had the responsibility of educating the next ruler, her daughter or son.

- She helped propagandize the monarchy by displays of pomp and beauty.

---

[2]Elizabeth A.R. Brown, "Eleanor of Aquitaine: Parent, Queen and Duchess," *Eleanor of Aquitaine: Patron and Politician*, William Kibler, ed. (Austin: University of Texas Press, 1976) p. 24.

[3]Joseph Dahmus, *Seven Medieval Queens* (New York: Doubleday, 1972), p. 241-275.

[4]Marion F. Facinger, "A Study of Medieval Queenship: Capetian France, 987-1237, *Studies in Medieval and Renaissance History*, Vol. V. William Bowsky, ed. (Lincoln: University of Nebraska Press, 1968), p.19.

As these many activities suggest, marriage for royalty had little to do with love and a great deal to do with power. Royal marriages were usually arranged when the participants were quite young, even infants. Royal marriages might serve several purposes. The most frequent was the dowry of money or land that came with the bride. For example, the non-royal Italian Medici family was able to marry two of their family members—Marie and Catherine—into the royal family of France because they promised enormous dowries. Anne of Brittany was a much sought-after bride because she brought with her this strategic territory between Britain and France. Religious motives might also be reasons for matrimony. In early times, good terms were frequently given in order that Christian queens would marry kings of areas not yet Christianized. The hope was that the queen's example would lead the kingdom to convert. For example, Queen Bertha, a Frankish princess, helped to bring Christianity to England.

Generally, the wives of kings were selected from other countries, partly to prevent the queen's family from influencing the court and partly to assure an outside alliance with a foreign country which might help to bolster militarily an unsure crown. Queens were expected to have influence back home, as, for example, when Catherine of Aragon wrote back to Spain for help with her husband's anti-French policies in the 16th century. Historians, examining the Anglo-Saxon past, have found that royal women were frequently expected to serve as peacemakers between warring tribes. Peace or war might depend upon their abilities to present their side of the quarrel.[5]

The queen might or might not be successful in bringing her new country benefits of land, money, and/or alliances. Sometimes, as in the case of Catherine of Aragon, all the dower money did not get paid and ugly wrangling resulted beween Henry VII of England and Ferdinand of Aragon. At other times, like the case of the Italian, Catherine de Medici, her assumption of power led to anti-Italian feelings instead of the alliance desired. But the geography of European nation states were shaped by royal marriages. The Hapsburg Empire, for example, was built from astute marriage alliances rather than wars of conquest.

Besides bringing political advantages by her marriages, the role of consort queen was to produce heirs to the throne. Some nations, such as France, did not allow women to inherit the throne. Heirs often meant sons, not daughters. Almost all biographies of royal women begin with the royal family eagerly awaiting a birth—and then the disappointment—a girl (or another girl).[6] The woman who could not have a son—and the woman was always blamed—was in a position of jeopardy. Despite the Roman Catholic Church's stand against divorce, annulment—the cancellation of a marriage by claiming marriage partners were too closely related—was sometimes possible. Since royal families frequently intermarried, this appeal to consanguinity, a blood relationship that was too close, was

_____

[5]Lorraine Lancaster, "Kinship in Anglo-Saxon Society-I," *British Journal of Sociology*, Vol. 9 (1958), p. 244.

[6]Some of these disappointments became the great rulers of their nations like Isabella of Spain, Elizabeth I of England or Catherine the Great of Russia.

an out in case no sons appeared. Examples of queens divorced for not giving birth to sons include Isabella Gomatrud, wife of John of England, Eleanor of Aquitaine[7] and Catherine of Aragon. Because their positions might depend on having sons, queens not only went on religious pilgrimages and ate special diets in hopes of becoming pregnant but also endangered their health to produce children. Queen Anne of England went through eighteen pregnancies without having a single living child. Four of the Capetian queens died in childbirth. But if the queen lived and had a son, her position in the court was strengthened. She had power first as consort queen and later as queen dowager for her son, the future king.

Besides alliances formed through marriage, dowries and heirs, queens also acted as backup power to their husband kings or, in Latin terms, "reglais imperii participes."[8] If the king did not wish to mediate events, he might send the queen as diplomatic ambassador.

One of the European wars ended with what has been called *The Ladies Peace*. Three women, Louise of Savoy, Margaret of Austria and Margaret of Navarre, negotiated the peace treaty.

In the days when kings were expected to lead their troops into battle and to fight in faraway crusades, the role of regent was a crucial one. The queen, left as regent for long periods of time, had to carry on the regular duties of king. When threatened, she had to organize the army as did Catherine of Aragon in Henry VIII's absence. Yolanda, another woman of Aragon, defended her husband's castles at Anjou and led troops into battle during his captivity. If the king were captured in battle, the regent queen and the dowager queen usually joined forces to get money for his release. Louise of Savoy and Margaret of Navarre bailed out Francis I of France; Blanche of Castile and Margaret of Provence sold their jewels for Louis IX's release and Richard the Lion Hearted might have remained imprisoned were it not for Eleanor of Aquitaine and Berengaria. Kings who were particularly weak and inept might rely on their wives. For example, the Merovingian King Clovis was "almost in a state of imbecility from the continual use of wine" and let his more able wife Bathilde be regent.[9] Henry VI of England had several breakdowns in mental health and his wife, Margaret of Anjou, acted for him. Holding on to a kingdom against powerful nobles required political ability. Sometimes the queen was successful; Yolanda held Anjou for the returning King Renee. But queens were not always able to control events. Yolanda's daughter Margaret lost England in the War of Roses although her son eventually reclaimed it.

If fighting off enemies and ransoming kings were some of the more demanding queenly duties, setting the tone of the court must have been a more pleasant task. A queen, by choosing her friends, chaplains, advisors, and entertainers, could often determine

---

[7]Eleanor of Aquitaine, however, had five sons by her next husband.

[8]H.G. Richardson and G.O. Sayles, *The Governance of Medieval England from the Conquest to Magna Carta* (Edinburgh: University Press, 1963), p. 153.

[9]Annie Forbes Bush, *Memoirs of the Queens of France* (Philadelphia: Carey & Hart, 1847), p. 68.

the cultural life of the court. Most queen's marriage contracts provided for an allowance of money; a queen might also have an income from her own lands. This often meant that she and the king were the major artistic patrons of the country. A queen more interested in frolic than philosophy might create a rather frivolous court. Anne of Denmark, wife of the English king, James I, for example, is accused by some historians (and defended by others) of lowering the high cultural level of Elizabeth I's court. The behavior of a really dissolute queen, like Isabella of Bavaria, Queen of France (one of whose crimes was to slit the throats of several legislators), led to such severe problems in France that a Joan of Arc was needed to solve them. However, by and large, the patronage of queens was a long and noble testimony of convents supported, churches built and hospitals begun with their donations. In days when the king's treasury was a household one, as in Capetian France, the queen's control of who was fed and given money meant that she was in charge of considerable social services.[10]

Besides supporting charity and the Church, queens also supported the literary and artistic works of many famous men and a few famous women of the period. Painters, like Rubens, won commissions from Marie de Medici of France. Writers like Rabelais dedicated parts of their works to the noted patron of the French Renaissance, Margaret of Navarre. A stormy debate among scholars centers on the influence of Eleanor of Aquitaine in fostering the courtly love tradition in both England and France. Troubadors certainly seemed to have been welcomed by her and the most famous, Christian de Troyes, dedicated his work on Lancelot to Marie de Champagne,

Eleanor's daughter. He said that the plot was Marie's idea, he just put it into verse..

Sometimes the tone of the court was particularly favorable for the advancement of women, especially when the queen was interested in their education. Catherine of Aragon's mother, Queen Isabella of Spain, had a strong belief in education for both sexes. Catherine's own court, with men like Juan Vives, Desiderius Erasmus and Thomas More, helped to create an atmosphere which encouraged classical education for women. Queen Anne of Brittany encouraged a sort of school for noble women so they could study seriously. Though a king might have more power and money for patronage, the consort queen could also shape the cultural history of a nation.

The consort queen might also play a major role in educating the next ruler. The queen's position was a focal one in the family loyalties. If there were stepsons, which was likely in days of high death rates, a queen might advance her own sons at the expense of her stepsons. One of the bloodier chapters of Merovingian French history is the story of the two rivals, Brunhild and Fredegunde who led armies into battle and killed enemies in order to place their sons on the throne. Even with her own son, the queen had to inspire enough admirable qualities to make him a good king. Yet she did not want to encourage his abilities so much that he became a rebellious subject while waiting to become king

---

[10]Facinger, p. 20.

through his father's death. Eleanor of Aquitaine became disgusted with her husband, Henry II, and let that duty slide. The result was a whole set of rebellious sons. One, Richard, was a better military leader than his father. Most queens, however, seemed to have tried to foster proper behavior in their sons. Blanche of Castile is generally credited with the moral upbringing that led her son to become the pious St. Louis (King Louis IX.) Another queen, Jeanne d'Albret of Navarre, wound up with a son who turned out to be one of the better kings of France, resolving religious civil war for a time. But, as this letter indicates, she advised him to shape up:

"I beg you, pay attention to three matters: be gracious, but speak boldly—set up an invincible resistance against this changing your religion and. . .try to train your hair to stand up and be sure there are no lice in it."[11]

Perhaps the most pleasurable duty of a consort queen was to share in the propaganda activities of the monarch. A good many puritanical subjects berated kings and queens for the extravagance of their dress and the cost of their jewels. Queens especially became the focus of this criticism, which was frequently true. Elizabeth I had 1000 gowns; Anne of England lost thousands of dollars playing cards. The poverty of peasant life appeared in stark contrast to the jeweled women of the court. More recent social historians, however, have stressed the value of dress and extravagant furnishings as part of the political attempt to show off the monarchy. Most queens were excellent horseback riders. This has been a royal tradition that continues through present times with Princess Anne, a member of the British Olympic equestrian team in the 1970's. Queens had to be able to ride well, not merely because kings often loved hunting, but because queens were expected to ride throughout the kingdom in the various processions and to demonstrate the elegance and wealth of the monarchy. These processions, as well as court entertainments of theater and dance, were designed to give visual, entertaining proof of the permanence and importance of the royal family. The image of a queen on the cover of a Gothic romance novel of today is often a jeweled woman decking herself out to glitter and enthrall. The reality of the medieval/Renaissance queen's life was that of pawning her jewels to pay for her husband's or brother's army, as did Margaret of Navarre. Isabella's selling her jewels for Columbus is part of a long tradition of jewels being sold for state use.

The duties of consort queens varied from era to era. There was more need for them to have military ability in the days of crusading kings. There was more need to know Latin at a time when the Renaissance stressed classical education. But many of their basic duties remained the same. Their fate might sometimes be violent death. A queen might be brutally executed like the Merovingian queen, Brunhild, who *"was tied to the tail of a wild horse, who dashed her brains out, and dragged her mangled body over rocks and stones."*[12]

---

[11]Nancy Lyman Roelker, *Queen of Navarre: Jeanne d'Albret 1528-1572* (Cambridge: Harvard University Press, 1968), p. 381.

[12]Bush, p. 62.

By Renaissance times, Henry VIII of England was civilized enough to send to France for an expert axman to chop off the head of his wife, Anne Boleyn. Most of the queen consorts managed to avoid the tragic end of Brunhild or Anne, though their duties were often complex and required courage.

The Reigning Queens— Queens Regina and Regent

The reigning queens—women who ruled in their own right or as lasting regents—did not fit the image of the ideal—quiet, submissive women. Indeed, there was some debate in medieval and Renaissance times about whether a reigning queen who married could really rule. Was not her duty to obey her husband? How could she then give orders which might contradict his wishes? It was a dilemma which drove poor Queen Mary I of England to near distraction. She had been raised with the ideal of the submissive, pious, Christian woman. She longed to preserve England as a Catholic country and, therefore had to assert herself as ruler. She was married to a man, King Philip II of Spain, who spent little time with her. Her letters pleaded for his return to England and for advice. Her sister, Elizabeth I, perhaps noting Mary's inner conflicts as wife and ruler, never married.[1] A later queen, Mary II, followed the first Mary's ideal and left statecraft to her husband William except for the times she served as regent.

Besides the question of whether a married queen or her husband should rule, there was the question as to whether a woman should rule at all. In some European nations, like England, women could inherit the throne only if there were no male

Queen Isabella I of Spain

heirs. Women could not inherit the throne in France. There is a good deal of controversy about the origins of this Salic law which declared that no woman could inherit the French throne. Some historians suggest that it was a misreading of early Merovingian laws that applied only to certain property. One biographer told the story of Queen Clothilde said to be so bloodthirsty that she decapitated the wife and children of an heir to the Burgundian throne, made the heir watch, then threw him down a well. This author states that after Clothilde's death in 568 A.D., the law against women inheriting the throne of France was introduced.[2] On the other hand, the Church was so impressed with Clothilde that they later designated her St. Clothilde.

---

[1] Or perhaps, seeing her father divorce two wives and cut off the heads of two more, Elizabeth did not have much faith in husbands.

[2] Annie Forbes Bush, *Memoirs of the Queens of France* (Philadelphia: Carey and Hart, 1847), p. 28.

Certain recent scholarship is more positive in evaluating this queen. There have been, then, differing historical views of Queen Clothilde and of her influence on the Salic Law. Some think that one reason that the Salic law lasted in France was that it did fit a commonly held view of women as inactive, incapable persons. John Knox, a Scots writer during the reign of Mary I of England, claimed that feminine rule was **"repugnant to nature...and the subversion of good order, equity and justice."**[3]

Despite all these reservations about women's ability to rule, monarchies in Europe have had ruling or regent queens for about one fourth of their history. France may have outlawed ruling queens, but its list of queen regents (and, later, kings' mistresses who ran state affairs) is a lengthy one. There were queens, like Jeanne d'Albret, who practiced religious freedom; her province of Navarre in France was the first European state to proclaim the right of religious toleration.[4] There were other queens less tolerant, like the regent Catherine de Medici, who was hated for encouraging the St. Bartholomew Massacre of Huguenots in France. There were queens noted for their stormy love lives and tragic endings, like that of Mary Queen of Scots who was executed as a traitor. Current historical novels and biographies mark the continued popular interest in these women's lives. Which of these many queens who ruled European monarchies for at least one quarter of their histories are considered the greatest? Most historians would probably select Isabella of Spain (r. 1474-1504) and Elizabeth I of England (r. 1558-1603).

These two queens have had much written about them, but a comparison might indicate their

Queen Elizabeth of England

Colonial Williamsburg Foundation

common concerns. Isabella faced the task of ruling a country, Castile, for which her uncle and brother had fought a bitter civil war. Elizabeth, too, faced the task of ruling a country divided on religious grounds—Protestant versus Catholic. In addition, both queens had to contend with nobles within, who wanted more power, and foreign enemies without. Both women shared a strong belief in the importance of having a classical education. Isabella struggled to learn Latin and to educate her children well; Elizabeth learned to speak Latin and Greek as well as French, Italian and German and to read available classical literature.

---

[3]Quoted in Joseph M. Levine, *Elizabeth I* (Englewood Cliffs: Prentice Hall, 1969), p. 21.

[4]Nancy Roelker, *Queen of Navarre: Jeanne d'Albret* (Cambridge: Harvard University Press, 1968), p. 225.

Both were women of physical courage. While pregnant, Isabella rode through Castilian hills, gathering together the Spanish army. Elizabeth often showed herself to crowds and stayed in London in times of emergency rather than finding more secure quarters. Both queens were interested in exploration. Isabella financed the first voyage of Columbus. Elizabeth also financed adventures in the Americas and her sailors reaped Spanish gold as pirates. Both queens accomplished their major goal. For Isabella this goal was the unification of Spain and for Elizabeth the maintenance of years of peace and prosperity which launched England as a world power.

These two queens can also be contrasted. Isabella believed strongly in her mission as a supreme defender of the Roman Catholic Church. In that role she, along with her husband Ferdinand, defeated the Muslim Moors, drove them from Spain and forced the Spanish Jews to leave Spain in exile. They began the Inquisition, whose aim was to uncover and remove heretics— Christians who were not followers of the Catholic faith. Isabella wanted a united and Catholic Spain. On the other hand, Elizabeth tried to prevent religious issues from erupting. She tried to discourage both Catholics and Protestant Puritans from upsetting the precarious balance of the Anglican Church.[5] The Anglicans (or Church of England) sought to keep some aspects of Catholicism while they maintained an independent, Protestant faith.

The two queens' lives were very different. Isabella was a devoted wife and mother. Elizabeth was a single woman whose affections revolved around several men but whose greatest loyalty was to her chief advisor, the able Lord Burghley. There was also a difference in their style of rule. Isabella set goals and followed them as steadfastly as she could. Elizabeth knew where she wanted to go but showed flexibility in changing policies to get there. One of her counselors despaired, *"No man can know the inward intention of her heart, but God and herself."*[6] Of herself, Elizabeth said if she was turned out of her realm she, *"could live in my petticoat."*[7] It was her wit, pragmaticism and wide ranging interests which made possible the era of history called Elizabethan England, which was the time of great writers such as Shakespeare, Marlowe, Bacon, Raleigh and Johnson.

Whatever their differences, both were recognized by their contemporaries as great queens. Isabella, aided by her warrior husband Ferdinand, prepared for the unification of Spain with administrative abilities equal to, if not greater than, Ferdinand's.[8] One of the sincerest compliments to Elizabeth—sincere because he hated her religious policies—came from the Catholic Pope: *"She certainly is a great Queen—just look how well she governs . . .*[9]

★ ★ ★ ★ ★ ★

[5]The Anglican Church, started by Henry VIII, Elizabeth's father.

[6]Quoted in Levine, p. 152.

[7]Quoted in Pearl Hogrefe, *Women of Action in Tudor England* (Ames: Iowa State University Press, 1977), p. 220.

[8]Ierne Plunket, *Isabel of Castile* (New York: G. P. Putnam's Sons, 1915).p. 387.

[9]Levine, p. 41.

If these two queens shaped policies that make their inclusion in traditional history books inevitable, what of all those consorts, regents or reginas, whose abilities as rulers were unquestioned but whose reigns did not involve such crucial events? To suggest what these queens were like, let us look at the Margarets.

One of the reasons that the history of late medieval and Renaissance queens becomes so confusing is that a very limited number of names were used. In early times, names were more distinctive such as those of the Merovingian queens, Radegonde and Calsunde and the Carolingian ones, Hermengmand and Gerberge. Later, certain names were used over and over. These queens, described here, were all named Margaret. All of them were relatively good rulers and so these Margarets suggest many of the roles female rulers played in medieval/Renaissance history.

St. Margaret of Scotland
(d. 1093): Although there is debate over how much influence St. Margaret had,[10] she is generally given credit for reviving the Catholic Church in IIth century Scotland, by endowing monasteries and encouraging learning.[11] She is said to have brought the more civilized customs of Europe to Scotland. Two of her children, Queen Maude I of England and David of Scotland, were known for their aid and piety to the Church.

Margaret of Denmark, Norway and Sweden (1353-1412)—Margaret had such extraordinary organizational ability that she nearly united the three Scandinavian countries of Denmark, Norway and Sweden. As the elected regent for these three areas, she managed to keep the Hanseatic League (the powerful trading association of Hanseatic cities of Northern Germany and nearby countries) from gaining more rights and privileges in Scandinavian countries. The empire she built did not last, but for a brief time was one of the largest in Europe.

Margaret of Anjou
(c. 1430-1482)—This Margaret was a battler. Her husband, Henry VI, suffered from breakdowns of mental health. England was in the midst of the War of the Roses and Margaret desired that her son be heir to the English throne. According to her biographers, she made mistakes because she did not understand the role of the English Parliament.[12] She also encouraged misguided French attacks against her English enemies.[13] Her energy in leading troops into battle and persistence in trying to gain allies, however, were remarkable.

Margaret of Austria
(1480-1530)—This Margaret was a ruler but never really a queen. It was intended that she be a queen; first betrothed to the French heir to the throne, that marriage fell through for political reasons. Then married to the Spanish heir, Isabella's son Juan, she was widowed. Forced into

[10]Derek Baker, "A Nursery of Saints: St. Margaret of Scotland Reconsidered," *Medieval Women* (Oxford: Basil Blackwell, 1978), p. 125.

[11] G.W.S. Barrow, 'From Queen Margaret to David I: Benedictines and Tironensians,' *Innes Review*, Vol. II (1960), p. 22-38.

[12]Philippe Erlanger, *Margaret of Anjou: Queen of England* (London: Elek Books, 1970), p. 149.

[13]Jock Haswell, *The Ardent Queen: Margaret of Anjou and the Lancastrian Heritage* (London: Peter Davies, 1976), p. 113.

marriage again, her second husband died as well. She then refused to be married off for a third time and instead, became ruler of the Netherlands. The reason hinged on a rather complicated set of circumstances. Isabella of Spain's daughter Joanna was found to be insane by her father, husband and son as they set out to rule Castile. Joanna's children, then, were taken from her and raised by Margaret, their aunt. One of Joanna's children became Emperor Charles V of the Hapsburgs, who ruled most of Europe. Needing someone he could trust, he asked his aunt to be regent for the Netherlands. She successfully ruled as regent for over twenty years, keeping the area secure and helping to negotiate peace settlements. A patron of the arts, Margaret was known as one of the most cultured women in Europe. She serves to illustrate that a royal woman's ability was an asset that able kings could well use.

Margaret of Valois (1553-1615)— Her reputation has been controversial. She was neither a virtuous widow nor a strong political leader and her personal conduct was thought rather daring. Through marrying Henry IV, she became queen of Navarre and later queen of France. Queen Margot (as she was called) and Henry were not a loving couple. Margaret rebelled and led a life that included various romantic love affairs. She was eventually exiled from Paris for her misbehavior. Henry IV tried to annul their marriage as he wished to marry his mistress but Queen Margot refused. Later, she consented to the annulment but set up her own small court or salon which encouraged talented writers and artists. She also wrote her memoirs and carried on a lively correspondence. Her life

illustrates both a certain sexual freedom with, in this case, an encouragement of the arts and a style that was a segment of some royal women's lives.

★ ★ ★ ★ ★ ★

These women do not exhaust the list of European Margarets who ruled. They do serve to suggest that the few great queens mentioned in usual history books were not there by accident but that, in reality, there were a great many female rulers. In the 1560's, for example, most of Europe was governed by women:

England . . . . Elizabeth
Scotland . . . . Mary Stuart
Portugal . . . daughter of Eleanor
Navarre . . . . Jeanne
The Low Countries . . . . . . Marie
Spain . . . . . . Isabella of France
France . . Catherine de Medici[14]

Margaret of Navarre
(1492-1549)—This woman was sometimes referred to as the Margaret of the Margarets.[15] There are some people in history whose reputations break through the barriers of time to find respect in other eras. She was one of these people. There are several reasons that she is remembered. One is her devotion to her brother, King Francis I. They really seemed to have liked one another. She went to Spain when he was captured to try to negotiate his release. In return, he protected her against accusations of

———————————

[14]Bush, Vol. I, p. 346.

[15]The name Margaret means pearl. Use of this phrase is a Renaissance play on words meaning that she was a pearl among pearls.

25

heresy. She is also remembered for her interest in Church reform and in the way that classical ideas related to the Bible. John Calvin, the Protestant reformer, was just one of many thinkers who sought sanctuary from religious persecution at her court.

Besides these qualities, she was interested in the arts, wrote a book of her own *The Heptameron Tales,* that some thought rather racy, and encouraged other writers like Rabelais. Above all, she was a strong role model for younger leaders. Her daughter, Jeanne d'Albret, and grandson, Henry IV, were influenced by her religious toleration. In her youth, Elizabeth I of England translated one of Margaret's pious books into Latin as a gift for her learned stepmother, Catherine Parr. While Margaret of Navarre was not without faults—for example, she forced a daughter into an unwanted marriage—she was, as one author put it, one of the outstanding forces of the French Renaissance.[16]

Musee Condé, Chantilly Giraudon Photograph

Queen Margaret of Navarre

---

[16]Samuel Putnam, *Marguerite of Navarre* (New York: Coward-McCann, 1935), p. 346.

Points to Consider

1. What were the four types of queens? How did they differ in the political power they might have?

   Why might there have been four types of queens, but only one king?

2. What is unusual about the roles Margaret of Denmark played?

3. What were some of the duties of the consort queen?

4. If a queen did not get along with the king, how could she use power against him? In what ways could she offer support to a threatened king?

5. Romantic love seems to be low on the list of requirements for these royal marriages. How might divorce be possible? What alternatives to divorce were there?

6. Extravagant jewels and dresses were often seen as royal women's vanity. What newer theories suggest other purposes for this display, expecially as it relates to queens?

7. Despite personal wealth and title, what duty was required of a queen consort who wished to retain her powerful position at court?

8. Salic law did not permit women to inherit property. How might this have become the principle that kept women from inheriting the throne of France?

9. In what ways can the reigns of Elizabeth I and Isabella of Spain be compared and contrasted?

10. The Margarets suggest that there was a whole group of successful women rulers. What were some of their achievements?

11. Why was Margaret of Navarre singled out as the most important of the Margarets?

12. Some historians have stated that England's most happy times have been with women rulers; England was at peace at home and protected abroad under rulers like Elizabeth I, Anne, Victoria and Elizabeth II. What effect may this history have had on the election of the first (of the major European powers) female Prime Minister, England's Margaret Thatcher?

13. In this chapter we looked closely at three roles of queens— Regina, Consort and Regent. Why might the role of Dowager Queen have been generally less influential than other roles for queens?

C. Women as Military Leaders

Christine de Pisan, one of the first women to become a professional writer, wrote a 15th century guide to proper behavior for women. In the section on a noblewoman's conduct, she offered the following advice:

"She [the lady of the castle] must. . .have the heart of a man; that is to know the law of arms and everything that belongs to them, so that she is ready to command her men if necessary in attack and defense, see that her fortresses are well provided. . ."[1]

Further advice to the lady of the castle included how to keep the loyalty of her barons and squires and how to raise taxes to pay for a war. The lady, in other words, had to be prepared to be a general. It was a preparation not usually found in any Christian woman's how-to-do-it handbook for living, but a necessary one for the Middle Ages.

It was necessary for several reasons. Feudalism was based upon the idea that the nobility gained land in exchange for military services to their ruler. These rulers often had only limited power and so nobles frequently were called upon to protect their own lands from other encroaching nobles. Sometimes however, a religious—or adventurous—spirit might sweep through Europe as it did in the late IIth century. Lords, knights and excess men would go off to the Crusades in the Middle East. Ideally, women were not supposed to crusade as they might tempt men from their religious vows of chastity and honor. Actually, many women, both rich and poor, did go on the

---

[1]Quoted in Ruth Kelso, *Doctrine for the Lady of the Renaissance* (Urbana: University of Illinois, 1956), p. 259.

Crusades (among them two queens of France, Eleanor of Aquitaine and Margaret of Navarre)[2] but most women remained at home. Often, nobles felt that only their wives could be trusted to protect, do battle and keep watch over their lands against others who might try to seize them while they were away at the Crusades. Accompanying this was always the possibility that the lady might become widowed, considering the high risk of death on the Crusades. In this case, the lady would frequently rule over the lands until a son or grandson came of age. For example, the Viscountess of Narbonne, Ermengarde, widowed twice, ruled her principality through both war and peace for sixty years.[3] Conducting warfare, then, was often a role of the lady.

Despite all the medieval talk of courtly love and chivalry, few nobles had any qualms about attacking a castle ruled by a woman. However, it might be somewhat embarrassing for the man to be beaten by the woman of the castle. Count Herbert, in 933 A.D., we are told, turned around and did not attack Lyon which was defended by the Duchess Ermine, *"fearing to be vanquished by a woman."*[4] However, most men did not hesitate to do battle with women leaders. Many romantic stories have resulted from incidents of ladies being attacked in their castles. One that seems true is that of the King of France, Louis IV who attacked the fortress at Luige in 939. The widow, Duchess Gerberge, organized a vigorous defense and held out through the siege. Louis, probably thinking he had found a woman of talent, decided to quit the siege and proposed marriage instead. She accepted and later defended some of Louis' fortresses when he was held prisoner.[5] Women defending their castles or mansions

Medieval Gate Tower

against outside attack was a common occurrence through the 17th century. We find, for example, Margaret Paston and her forces in 1450, holding out against 1000 men and Lady Brilliana Harley defending her castle in the 16th century English Civil War.[6]

Women leaders not only defended their property with military means but also went on the attack. Alfred the Great is remembered for uniting England following the disruptions of

[2]Marion Meade, *Eleanor of Aquitaine* (New York: Hawthorn Books. 1977). p. 72.

[3]Emily James Putnam, *The Lady* (Chicago: University of Chicago Press, 1969) (1910), p. 130.

[4]Annie Forbes Bush, *Memoirs of the Queens of France*, Vol. I (Philadelphia: Carey and Hart, 1847), p. 100.

[5]*Ibid.*, p. 101-102.

[6]Pearl Hogrefe, *Tudor Women: Commoners and Queens* (Ames: Iowa State University Press, 1975), p. 68, 74.

invasions caused by the Danish. Yet, it was his two children, Edward and Aethelflaed, who added even more territory to England than Alfred had. Aethelflaed, the Lady of the Mercians, matched the territorial expansion of her father by leading troops against the Danes, winning new land and then building fortifications to protect this added territory.[7]

Another woman whose military actions had a major effect on a nation's history was Matilda of Tuscany. She became involved in the war between the Holy Roman Emperor, Henry IV, and Pope Gregory VII. It was her armies—led by her—which helped to protect Rome. Although she eventually married, some Catholic historians have referred to her as "the warrior maid of the Holy Church."[8] She continued to spend time embroiled in military adventures—she even kept two suits of armor readied for battle.[9] Many history books show paintings of the famous meeting of Henry coming to Canossa to beg forgiveness from the Pope. But few books mention Matilda who fought to protect the Pope and whose territory included Canossa.

There were many other women in European history like Aethelflaed and Matilda. For example, there was Yolanda of Aragon, who "went out on a white charger"[10] and protected Anjou from attack for her son, Louis III. Yolanda's granddaughter, Margaret, shared her ability to raise and encourage troops in an attempt to keep the English throne for her son. It was Yolanda who helped convince the Daulphin of France to heed Joan of Arc's plan to drive the British out of France. The army that accompanied Joan was one raised in part by Yolanda who had both the ability and experience to do it.[11] To raise an army took both charisma

and physical endurance. When Isabella of Spain raised the army that she and Ferdinand used to drive the Moors from Spain, she traveled on horseback throughout the country gathering men. One scholar has said that her "incessant mobility almost makes one seasick" just to read her letters, so constantly was she on the move.[12] The creation of this army was really her achievement. In Italy, Caterina Srorza fought many battles to preserve her duchy. She finally lost it to Desare Borgia. She was the only Sforza family member who did not try to escape but stayed to do battle.[13]

As so many were involved in warfare, it was inevitable that women would sometimes fight one another. *The War of the Three Ladies* took place in 14th century France in dispute over lands. These three were Jeanne de Montfort, Jeanne de Clisson and Jeanne de Penthieure, all trying to secure lands claimed by their sons or husbands. Jeanne de Montfort was called "the most extraordinary woman of the age"[14]

---

[7]Richard Humble, *The Fall of Saxon England* (London: Arthur Barker, 1975), p. 92-93.

[8]Nora Duff, *Matilda of Tuscany* (NY: E. F. Dutton, 1910), p. 8.

[9]*Ibid.*, p. 77.

[10]Edgcumbe Staley, *King Rene D'Anjou and His Seven Queens* (London: John Long, 1912), p. 82.

[11]Philippe Erlanger, *Margaret of Anjou: Queen of England* (London: Elek Books, 1970), p. 44-45.

[12]Townsend Miller, *The Castles and the Crown: Spain 1451-1555* (NY: Coward-McCann, 1963), p. 122.

[13]Ernst Breisach, *Caterina Sforza: A Renaissance Virago* (Chicago: University of Chicago Press, 1967), p. 210.

[14]David Hume quoted in Pierce Butler, *Women of Medieval France* (Philadelphia: Rittenhouse Press, 1907), p. 302.

for her wit and daring. We know some details of her abilities from the writings of the French historian Froissart. Here is her speech as recorded by Froissart with a description of the actions she took to maintain the loyalty of her vassals during her husband's imprisonment.

" '*Ah! sirs, be not cast down because of my lord, whom we have lost: he was but one man. See here my little child, who shall be, by the grace of God, his restorer [avenger] and who shall do well for you. I have riches in abundance, and I will give you thereof and will provide you with such a captain that you shall all be comforted.' When she had thus comforted her friends and soldiers in Rennes, then she went to all her other fortresses and good towns, and led ever with her John her young son, and did to them as she did at Rennes, and fortified all her garrisons of everything that they wanted, and paid largely and gave freely, whereas she thought it well employed.*"

These are some of Froissart's descriptions of how she organized the defense of Hennebon and one or her other exploits.

"*When the countess and her company understood that the Frenchmen were coming to lay siege to the town of Hennebon, then it was commanded to sound the watch-bell alarm, and every man to be armed and draw to their defense.*"

After some preliminary skirmishes, in which the French lost more than the Bretons, Charles's army encamped for the night about Hennebon. Next day the siege began with minor attacks, followed on the third day by a general assault.

"*The Countess herself, wearing armor, rode on a great war horse from street to street, desiring her people to make good defence, and she caused women to tear up the pavements of the streets and carry stones to the battlements to cast upon their enemies, and great pots full of quicklime.*

"*The Countess de Montfort did here a hardy feat of arms, and one which should not be forgotten, She had mounted a tower to see how her people fought and how the Frenchmen were ordered without. She saw how that all the lords and all other people of the host were all gone out of their field to the assault. Then she bethought her of a great feat, and mounted once more her war horse, all armed as she was, and caused three hundred men a-horseback to be ready, and went with them to another gate where there was no assault. She and her company sallied out, and dashed into the camp of the French lords, and cut down tents and fired huts, the camp being guarded by none but varlets and boys, who ran away. When the Lords of France looked behind them and saw their lodgings afire and heard the cry and noise there, they returned to the camp crying 'Treason! treason!' so that all the assault was left.*

"*When the Countess saw that, she drew together her company, and when she saw that she could not enter again into the town without great damage, she went straight away toward the castle of Brest, which is but three leagues from there. When Sir Louis of Spain, who was marshal of the host, was come to the field, and saw their lodgings burning and the Countess and her company going away, he followed after her with a great force of men at arms. He chased her so near that he slew and hurt divers of them that were behind, evil horsed; but the Countess and the most part of her company rode so well that they came to Brest, where they were received with great joy by the townspeople.''*[15]

★ ★ ★ ★ ★ ★

After a great naval battle this same Countess Jeanne de Montfort was described:

"The Countess that day was worth a man; she had the heart of a lion, and in her hand she wielded a sharp glaive [sword], where with she fought fiercely.''[16]

How did husbands who were away or captured feel about their wives taking command? Most probably felt grateful, particularly after they were returned home or were released from prison. The Great Conde, famous French general, noted the contrast of his life with that of his wife during his rather genteel imprisonment. He said, *"Isn't it strange that my wife should be carrying on war while I water the garden?"*[17]

The Lady of the manor hunts using falcons during her leisure time

Some of these women, like the Renaissance leader Caterina Sforza (c. 1462-1509), matched the ruthlessness of any male Borgia while other women combined the worlds of diplomacy and war more admirably. The following is a description of the late medieval female Irish leader, Inion Dubh, who was part of a council of war:

"It was an advantage that she came to the gathering for she was the head of advice and counsel of the Cenel Conaill, and though she was calm and very deliberate and much praised for her womanly qualities, she had the heart of a hero and the mind of a soldier. . . . She had many troops from Scotland, and some of the Irish at her disposal and under her control, and in her own hire and pay constantly, and especially during the time that her son was in prison and confined by the English.''[18]

The Irish also had other women leaders and even a pirate queen, called Grainne Mhaol during the reign of Elizabeth I of England.

In the medieval period there was a real need for women with military leadership ability. Joan of Arc was part of this tradition. Though the most famous of these figures, she differed from them in several ways.

[15]*Ibid.*, p. 293.

[16]*Ibid.*, p. 294-295.

[17]Quoted in Mrs. Alfred Cock, *The Life of Madame de Longueville* (London: Smith, Elder and Company, 1899), p. I06.

[18]Katharine Simms, ''Women in Norman Ireland,'' in *Women in Irish Society in Historical Dimension,* Margaret MacCurtain and Donncha O'Corrain, eds, (Westport: Greenwood Press, 1979), p. 18.

Most of the women mentioned in this chapter were women of the nobility, fighting to defend their realms or specific property. Joan came from the lower classes and fought for her nation, France. She believed that she was inspired by God. Without the protection of being one of the nobility and thus open to the charge of being a heretic, Joan's fate was to be burned at the stake.[19] All these women, including Joan, demonstrate that physical courage and strategic ability were not confined to the male gender.

Points to Consider

1. For what specific reasons could military ability be an expected part of being a lady?

2. In what sort of military activities did women engage?

3. In what ways was Joan of Arc both part of a tradition and an exception to it?

---

[19]Joan of Arc's history is a fascinating one—it appears in readily available biographies. Of these Edward Lucie-Smith, *Joan of Arc* (New York: W.W. Norton Co., 1976) is one of the most recent and readable.

Chapter 2
Religious Women in Medieval/Renaissance Europe

A. Women in the Roman Catholic Church
The Active Nuns

The 19th century British poet Wordsworth referred to a pastoral, country scene as being "quiet as a nun." He (like many of his early 19th century contemporaries) would have thought of a pious, black-cowled nun, praying with down-turned eyes. In the 1960's and 70's, this quiet image was challenged by nuns in the United States who dressed in modern clothes, joined protest marches in the streets and demanded more rights within the Roman Catholic Church hierarchy. To answer those critical of modern nuns for breaking with tradition, Church women could say that they were following medieval nuns' traditions of activism. The history of women in the Roman Catholic Church has been one filled with activity and controversy.

One of the first controversies involved what was to be the role of women in the Church. In his teachings, Jesus made no distinctions between male or female souls. Although his disciples were male, he had encouraged women like Mary, Martha and Mary Magdalen to spread his teachings. Later, St. Paul had discouraged Christian women from speaking in the Church, but had relied on women like Lydia to spread the gospel. He had also encouraged her to be an active disciple in his letters. Various sects within Christianity such as the Gnostic, had stressed the female aspect of God and allowed women to act as priests.[1] In the early Church, there seems to have been a respected role of preacher/teacher, but this role was not exclusively male or female. For example, an early Christian fresco (wall painting) in Rome shows women serving

---

[1]Elaine Pagels, *The Gnostic Gospels* (New York: Random House, 1979), p. 60.

the bread and wine to commemorate the mass.[2] Other mosaics show women bishops of the early Church; dedications of Roman archaeological remains suggest women's priestly roles.[3] However, at the Council of Laodices in 352 A.D. (one of many councils called to decide proper church doctrine) it was decided that women could not be priests.[4] After this decision, only male priests had the right to say mass, preach and hear confession. Female nuns, in theory at least, could not perform these rituals and duties.

What, then, would be the role of women in the Church? St. Paul seems to have suggested a religious order of nuns made up of older widows;[5] other church officials preferred orders formed of nuns of all ages. Could these women marry? Could male priests marry? These were hotly debated issues. The early Christian Church stressed a vow of virginity as a heroic measure against sin and as a focus of one's life exclusively upon the Church. By the 4th century, marriages of nuns were condemned as *"more sinful than adultery."*[6] The Church also discouraged the marriage of priests but this was not enforced until a Church council of the 10th century was held. By the 5th century, the role of a nun was a religious woman who took a vow of chastity and whose duty was to the Church, not to people of the congregation. Other questions remained concerning nuns—who could be a nun and what were her religious duties?

Though any woman might become a nun, in theory, the general practice in the medieval period was that nuns came from the upper class. Since convents or monasteries[7] were supposed to be self-supporting, nuns brought dowries of money or land to help maintain the convent during most of the medieval period. Women were not legally required to bring dowries with them, but most did so. Later orders, like the Beguines and Poor Clares, included some women without dowries from the lower classes.[8] The abbesses, or leaders of the convents, were often appointed because of their connection with the court or wealthy nobility. In the 10th century, when the daughter of Otto I of the Holy Roman Empire became a nun, she was made abbess and had jurisdiction over several cities and the power of a bishop.[9] At times, a widowed wife of a king or noble would retire to a convent to become a nun or take over the duties of abbess. These women brought to convents important social connections outside the Church and often had held responsible positions in powerful households before becoming nuns.

[2]Joan Morris, *The Lady Was A Bishop* (New York: Macmillan Co., 1973), p. 5.

[3]Lecture by: Dr. Dorothy Irban, Professor of Theology, St. Catherine College, St. Paul, MN.

[4]Henry C. Lea, An Historical Sketch of Sacerdotal Celibacy in the Christian Church (Cambridge: Houghton Mifflin Co., 1884) p. 59.

[5]*Ibid.*, p. 95-96.

[6]*Ibid.*, p. 103-104.

[7]Ernest McDonnell, *The Beguines and Beghards in Medieval Culture* (New Brunswick: Rutgers, 1954), p. 535. The names were used interchangeably for place of religious retreat and housed both male and female, for example "double monasteries" of Kildarc Abbey in Ireland. Aubrey Gwynn and R. Neville Hadcock, *Medieval Religious Houses: Ireland* (London: Longman's 1970), p. 307.

[8]Eileen Power, *Medieval English Nunneries* (Cambridge: Cambridge University Press, 1922), p. 16.

[9]Morris, p. 58.

What motives did women have for becoming nuns? Many, perhaps most, did so because they were religious and wished to serve God in that manner. One Anglo-Saxon queen, Aethelthrith, left her royal husband and her kingdom in 673 to begin a convent where *"men and women readily flock thither to live under the guidance of the queen."*[10] The lives of the saints, many who were nuns, testify to the deep religious feelings of women in the Church. Some women did become nuns because it offered more freedom than another sort of life might give them.[11] In medieval times, married life could have considerable drawbacks. One medieval writer pictured the contrast between married life and convent life as follows:

"And how I ask, though it may seem odious, how does the wife stand who when she comes in hears her child scream, sees the cat stealing food, and the hound at the hide? Her cake is burning on the stone hearth, her calf is sucking the milk, the earthen pot is overflowing into the fire. Though it be an odious tale, it ought, maiden, to deter thee more strongly from marriage, for it does not seem easy to her who has tried it. Though, happy maiden, who hast fully removed thyself out of that servitude as a free daughter of God and as His Son's spouse, needest not suffer anything of the kind."[12]

The convent, on the other hand, often seemed a peaceful place of learning when contrasted to the distractions of running a home. The German nun, Lioba, a dedicated intellectual, *"never laid aside her books except to pray—or eat or sleep."*[13]

Convents might also offer a comparatively comfortable life. Al-

The Nuns' kitchen at the Abbey of Fontrevault, France

though some convents were poor, particularly in the decline of the 13th and 14th centuries,[14] the better endowed institutions had fairly high standards of living, especially for the abbess. For example, bishops visiting some of the English nunneries were disconcerted to discover nuns dressing in colorful clothes, painting their faces, wearing fur on their gowns, eating delicate foods, bringing their dogs into

[10]Lina Eckenstein, *Woman Under Monasticism* (Cambridge: Cambridge University Press, 1896), p. 96.

[11]Emily Putnam, *The Lady* (Chicago: University of Chicago Press, 1969), (1910), p. 69-105.

[12]Eckenstein, p. 327.

[13]*Ibid.*, p. 137.

[14]Sally Thompson, "The Problem of the Cistercian Nuns in the 12th and 13th Centuries," *Medieval Women,* Derek Baker, ed. (Oxford: Basil Blackwell, 1978), p. 251.

church and even letting their pet monkeys swing about.[15] One abbess was told that she might have no more than two maid servants, which suggests that her life was spent neither in silence nor hard labor.[16] Life in a medieval nunnery also did not mean being hidden from the world. Though priests, bishops and popes tried again and again to enclose or shut in nuns, nuns continued to go on pilgrimages, visit relatives or other convents, and see to the business of the land owned by the abbey or convent.[17]

While some women entered the convent for religious or social reasons, some others entered because they were forced. One of the problems of having daughters in medieval and Renaissance periods was that the family was expected to furnish a dowry upon a young woman's marriage. The bigger the dowry, the more likely that a better marriage would result—one that might benefit the family. If there were several daughters in the family, one or two were sometimes sent to a convent so that the other daughter might have a larger dowry and so be able to marry upward into a more powerful family. One German duke—no doubt impoverished—sent all nine of his daughters to a convent so he would not have to worry about large dowries for any of them.[18] Some dowry money had to be paid to the convent, but this might only be maintenance money and not a great sum. During certain periods in medieval Italy, when marriage dowry rates became competitively high, many women were forced into convents against their will.[19] By the late Middle Ages, these convents were criticized as *"elegant clubs for surplus daughters of the nobility."*[20] Some women, physically handicapped and not likely prospects for the rather brutal

marriage market system of the day, were sent to convents. As one said, rather bitterly, *"I was not good enough for man, and so am given to God."*[21] Illegitimate daughters also made poor marriage bargains and were sometimes sent to convents.

Not all women who were sent against their will to nunneries went easily. Some tried secret marriages, others threatened suicide or used other means to make their protest. When her Aunt Christiana tried to get Maud, later Good Queen Maud of England, to wear a veil in anticipation of her becoming a nun, Maud rebelled: *"I did indeed wear [it] in her presence, but as soon as I was able to escape out of her sight, I tore it off and threw it on the ground and trampled on it . . ."*[22] Employing the nunneries as a storehouse of excess women was probably the most damaging action taken toward the convents as it created a disharmony of aims for the women there. The religious women wished piety. Those forced into the convent life wished more worldliness.

---

[15]Power, p. 61.

[16]*Ibid.*, p. 61.

[17]Eileen Power, *Medieval People* (New York: Harper and Row, 1963), p. 93. Her essay "Madame Eglentyne" included in this book is an excellent, readable one on English nuns.

[18]Marcelle Bernstein, *The Nuns* (New York: Bantam Press, 1976), p. 47.

[19]John Addington Symonds. *Renaissance in Italy*, (London: Smith, Elder & Co., 1909), p. 245.

[20]Margaret Trouncer, *The Reluctant* Abbess: Angelique Arnauld of Port Royal (New York: Sheed and Ward, 1957), p. 34.

[21]Power, *Medieval English Nunneries*, p. 31.

[22]Derek Baker, "A Nursery of Saints," *Medieval Women*, p. 123-124.

By the late 17th century certain women had doubts about allowing their daughters to go to convents, fearing that there had been a falling away from previous standards. Madam de Sevigne wrote to her daughter about her granddaughter's possible admission to a convent.

"Ah, my child, keep her with you! She will never get a good education in a convent, neither in religion (of which the nuns know very little) nor in anything else...At home she could read good books...for her taste lies that way; you could discuss them with her...I am sure that would be much better than a convent."[23]

Once a woman became a nun, whether by choice or force, what were her duties? Basically she had two sets of duties—one as a participant in religious services and another as an assigned role within the convent community. Religious duties might differ depending upon which order of nuns a woman joined. Some nuns, like the Beguines, lived in small houses within cities and had simple morning and evening prayer services. Other nuns were more enclosed and lived a life of constant prayer. Benedictine rules of convent life called for a daily schedule usually like this:

Choir nuns singing

2:00 A.M.	—up to go into the church to say Matins, Lauds
6:00 A.M.	—up to go into church, say Prime
8:00 A.M.	—Tierce: prayers
10:00 A.M.	—Sext: prayers
12:00 Noon	—None: prayers
5:00 P.M.	—Vespers: prayers
7:00 P.M.	—Campline: prayers Bed[24]

Between prayers, nuns were expected to keep busy with housekeeping duties. The kinds of chores a nun did depended on assigned tasks within the abbey or convent. In addition to nuns, the abbey also housed many non-nuns who also worked at convent tasks. Lands around the abbey donated for its support, had to be farmed; sheep on the land had to be raised and slaughtered for food. Even law cases had to be carried on to protect the abbey's rights. Sometimes quarrels broke out over the collection of church tithes (taxes) as when an Italian priest accused the local Cistercian nuns of stealing *"Two oxen and one steer, three sows and four hogs, besides a quantity of hay, chestnuts, wheat and nuts."*[25] These abbeys

---

[23]Quoted in Brink, p. 108.

[24]Powers, *Medieval English Nunneries*, p. 79.

[25]Catherine Boyd, *A Cistercian Nunnery in Medieval Italy* (Cambridge: Harvard University Press, 1943), p. 66

were often like small villages or towns and as such the center of local economic activity. Because of their importance, nuns who administered them often held a variety of duties. The following chart suggests a number of roles in a powerful abbey:[26]

Abbess

Administered the Abbey

In case of a double monastery, this meant to direct the monks as well as nuns

Acted as spiritual leader: sometimes the abbess also acted as confessor and might preach

Called out troops if the ruler required it

Collected taxes and tithes (payments to the church)

Maintained the buildings

Initiated legal cases

Selected chaplains and priests for the nuns' order from local churches

Encouraged scholarship

Supervised children in the convent schools

Educated missionaries

Fatress

Kept the rectory (living quarters) clean
Repaired chairs and tables
Supervised table settings
Saw that the lavatory was clean

Sacrist[27]

Cared for the church sanctuary
Polished silverplate
Kept vestments (robes uses in services)
Directed the creation and maintenance of altar cloths
Supervised the making of candles for the sanctuary

Cellaress

Was in charge of food supply for the nuns and servants; ordered ale, grain for bread, pickled meat and bought fish

Chantress

Managed church services
Trained nuns for singing
Acted as librarian

Infirmaress

Was in charge of the sick—bathed them, changed beds, and gave medicine

Chambress

Was in charge of every day clothing
Saw to the repair and making of clothes

Treasuress

Received all money paid to the abbey
Paid all bills
Kept account records
Planned yearly budget

Mistress of Novices

Was school mistress to the novices (student nuns)
Oversaw the proper behavior of members of the order

Kitchenness

Supervised fixing of the meals

Almoness

Dispersed alms to poor

[26]Morris, p. 16.

[27]These categories are representative of English nunneries: See Power, *Medieval English Nunneries*, p. 131-160.

A glimpse at the extent to which these women had to plan and organize may be seen in the following quotation from a l4th century abbess. She related the budgeting of different lands for different purposes.

". . .For bread and beer—produce of land and tennants in Tilney, half church of St. Peter in Wiggenhall. . .Produce of land in Gyddergore. . .houses and rents in Lynn and in North Lynn and in Gaywood for meat and fish and herring. For clothing and shoes all the produce of our meadow in Setchy. . .and the remnant of the land in Setchy and West Winch is ordained for the purchase of salt. . .For tablecloths, towels and other things which are needed for guests and for the household. . . produce of our land and tenements in Thorpland. . . Similarly the breeding of stock, and all the profits which may be drawn from our beasts in Tilney, in Wiggenhall and in Thorpland, and In all other places (saving the stock for our larder, and draught-beasts for carts and ploughs and saving four-and-twenty cows and a bull) are assigned and ordained for the repair of new houses and new dykes, to the common profit of the house."[28]

While their religious commitment may have been otherworldly, nuns, because of their social standing and economic power, were also factors in worldly affairs. They were often conscious of their role in this wider world outside the convent. Educated nuns often had extensive correspondence with leading intellectual figures of their day. Hildegard, Abbess of a convent at Bingen, Germany, wrote philosophical treatises and traveled widely in Europe to share her scholarship. Like other medieval scholars, her view of the world as a sphere anticipated Renaissance findings.[29] Another nun, Hroswitha, was known for the plays she wrote in Latin.

Nuns also could be firm about what they saw to be their rights. A dispute over who was to be abbess, for example, caused a revolt in Poitiers Abbey in the 6th century that lasted for two years. There were troops of men—and nuns—that fought on both sides of this dispute.[30] When the Church tried to limit the power of these abbesses or tried to place bishops or abbots over them, rebellions took place throughout Europe. For example, one abbot excommunicated a whole Cistercian nunnery. His action was futile since these nuns told him he had no right to oversee the abbey and locked the doors against him.[31] Sometimes an abbey would appeal its case to Rome and the Pope would allow the abbey its own rights.[32] Even if they admitted that the bishop had jurisdiction over them, they did not necessarily feel they had to take his advice. A bishop

---

[28]*Ibid.*, p. 134-135.

[29]Linda Saport, "Scientific Achievements of Nuns in the Middle Ages," Unpublished Paper, November 25, 1978, p. 7.

[30]Eckenstein, p. 66-67.

[31]Excommunicate: deny all access to religious rites.

[32]Boyd, p. 116.

An Abbess carries a crosier in a procession.

in the role of a local lord, with large lands to administer and duties to the king. In taking part in the events of their own day as well as maintaining their religious commitment, medieval nuns and modern nuns share a common heritage.

came to the English nunnery, Markyate, in 1300 A.D. to tell the nuns that Pope Boniface VIII had enclosed these nuns so that *"on pain of excommunication no nun or sister could go outside the bounds of the monastery."* The nuns took the statute of the decree, threw it at the bishop as he left and told him *"they were not content in any way to observe such a statute."*[33] Threats of excommunication did not end the nuns'objections to being enclosed. During the next three centuries bishops repeatedly sent reports to the Popes at Rome that nuns were still traveling, boarding outsiders, taking pilgrimages and entertaining guests at the convent.

Nuns of the medieval period, then, led lives more complex than quiet. They often provided social services such as hospitals, overnight hostels, schools, as well as giving charity to the peoples of the surrounding countryside. The abbess often acted

Points to Consider

1. In what ways were the medieval nuns not always quiet nor merely pious?

2. The role of abbess differed in various eras, but what generally were some of her responsibilities?

3. What types of women became nuns?

   In what specific ways might the role of nun be attractive even to a non-religious woman?

   What might be some limitations to the role of nun in medieval times?

---

[33] Quoted in Power, *Medieval English Nunneries.* p. 352.

B. Mystics as Activists
Four Female Saints

Introduction

One group of women in medieval/Renaissance times stands out in history, is frequently represented in literature and known for its vital religious leaders. These women were canonized[1]. After their deaths—they were declared saints of the Roman Catholic Church. Occasionally, even in modern times, the Roman Catholic Church has canonized both men and women.[2] However, from the time of early Christianity to the Reformation in the 17th century, these spiritual people were often outstanding political or social reformers. Therefore, these female saints have been admired not only for their spirituality, but also for their influence on the affairs of their day. In early medieval times some dedicated, saintly women became missionaries in order to convert pagan tribal people, such as the Saxons in northern Europe, to Christianity. Later, other women became the respected advisors to bishops and Popes and often worked for church reforms. Finally, some of these saints came to play important political roles by advising kings and queens.

The following are short sketches of four of these female saints. They were chosen as being representative from the many important female saints of medieval/Renaissance times. In reading about their lives,

_____

[1]After an extensive investigative process to determine the deserving qualities of the person—often including special signs of holiness—the Roman Catholic Church officially canonizes or declares the person as saint sometime after their death.

[2]For example, an American woman (Elizabeth Seton, 1774-1826, known as Mother Seton) was declared a saint in 1980.

think of the following questions:

- In what specific ways do these women seem similar? Different?
- How did they influence their own times?
- What seems to be especially holy about them that might explain why they were canonized by the Catholic Church?

Saint Lioba

Early medieval England of Lioba's time (c. 700-779) was already Christianized. The Anglo-Saxon peoples of England had been converted by missionaries sent around 590 by Pope Gregory the Great. However, large areas of continental Europe were still held by tribal peoples who kept to pagan beliefs. Lioba's life spanned part of the reign of Charlemagne (768-814) who first united much of Europe under one Christian rule. One tribal group remaining pagan in the 8th century was that of the Germans of Saxony. Lioba was sent by Bishop Saint Boniface to administer one of the convents set up in Saxony. There she converted tribal peoples to the Christian faith and founded religious orders to continue the work of converting these pagans. Selections follow from the *Life of Saint Lioba* written some 50 years after her death by the learned monk, Rudolf. Although the aim of Rudolf's account of her life was probably meant to provide spiritual inspiration,[3] a sense of the real woman, Lioba, is present in his biography.

Rudolf's account begins with Lioba's birth into a comfortably well-off noble English family of Wessex:

"As we have already said, her parents were English, of noble family and full of zeal for religion and the observance of God's commandments. Her father was called Dynno, her mother Aeba. But as they were barren, they remained together for a long time without children. After many years had passed and the onset of old age had deprived them of all hope of offspring, her mother had a dream in which she saw herself bearing in her bosom a church bell, which on being drawn out with her hand, rang merrily. When she woke up she called her old nurse to her and told her what she had dreamt. The nurse said to her: 'We shall yet see a daughter from your womb and it is your duty to consecrate her straightway to God. So you must offer her, when she has been taught the Scripture from her infancy, to serve Him in holy virginity as long as she shall live.' Shortly after the woman had made this vow she conceived and bore a daughter, surnamed Lioba."

Even as a child, Lioba was said to have had a special interest and aptitude for a spiritual life:

"... The girl, therefore, grew up and was taught with such care by the abbess and all the nuns that she had no interests other than the monastery and the pursuit of sacred knowledge. She took no pleasure in aimless jests and wasted no time on girlish romances, but, fired by the love of Christ, fixed her mind always on reading or hearing the Word of God. Whatever she heard or read she committed to memory, and

---

[3]Eleanor McLaughlin, "Women, Power and The Pursuit of Holiness in Medieval Christianity," in *Women of Spirit,* Rosemary Ruether and Eleanor McLaughlin, eds, (New York: Simon and Schuster, 1979) p. 103-l04.

put all that she learned into practice. She exercised such moderation in her use of food and drink...[and] she prayed continually.... When she was not praying she worked with her hands at whatever was commanded her..."

The Anglo-Saxon priest, Saint Boniface, had been sent by the Pope to Saxony in northern Germany to convert the pagan tribal people. Boniface sent for Lioba to be an abbess to a group of German nuns, because she had already gained a reputation for scholarship and holiness:[4]

"He gave her the monastery at a place called Bischofsheim, where there was a large community of nuns. These were trained according to her principles in the discipline of monastic life and made such progress in her teaching that many of them afterwards became superiors of others, so that there was hardly a convent of nuns in that part which had not one of her disciples as abbess. She was a woman of great virtue and was so strongly attached to the way of life she had vowed that she never gave thought to her native country or her relatives. She extended all her energies on the work she had undertaken in order to appear blameless before God and to become a pattern of perfection to those who obeyed her in word and action."

Rudolf explains wonderful events relating to her, "God had performed many miracles through Lioba."

The Miracle of the Fire

"On another occasion, when she sat down as usual to give spiritual instruction to her disciples, a fire broke out in a part of the village. As the houses have roofs of wood and thatch, they were soon consumed by the flames, and the conflagration spread with increasing rapidity towards the monastery, so that it threatened to destroy not only the buildings but also the men and beasts. Then could be heard the mingled shouts of the terrified villagers as they ran in a mob to the abbess and begged her to avert the danger which threatened them. Unruffled and with great self control, she calmed their fears and, without being influenced by their trust in her, ordered them to take a bucket and bring some water from the upper part of the stream that flowed by the monastery. As soon as they had brought it, she took some salt which had been blessed by Saint Boniface and which she always kept by her, and sprinkled it in the water. Then she said: 'Go and pour back this water into the river and then let all the people draw water lower down the stream and throw it on the fire.' After they had done this the violence of the conflagration died down and the fire was extinguished just as if a flood had fallen from the skies. So the buildings were saved. At this miracle the whole crowd stood amazed and broke out into praise of God, who through the faith and prayers of his handmaid had delivered them so extraordinarily from a terrible danger."

---

[4]*Ibid.*, p. 104.

The Miracle of the Storm

"I think it should be counted amongst her virtues also that one day, when a wild storm arose and the whole sky was obscured by such dark clouds that day seemed turned into night, terrible lightning and falling thunderbolts struck terror into the stoutest hearts and everyone was shaking with fear. At first the people drove their flocks into the houses for shelter so that they should not perish; then, when the danger increased and threatened them all with death, they took refuge with their wives and children in the church, despairing of their lives. They locked all the doors and waited there trembling, thinking that the last judgment was at hand. In this state of panic they filled the air with the din of their mingled cries. Then the holy virgin [Lioba] went out to them and urged them all to have patience. She promised them that no harm would come to them; and after exhorting them to join with her in prayer, she fell prostrate at the foot of the altar. In the meantime the storm raged, the roofs of the houses were torn off by the violence of the wind, the ground shook with the repeated shocks of the thunderbolts, and the thick darkness, intensified by the incessant flicker of lightning which flashed through the windows, redoubled their terror. Then the mob, unable to endure the suspense any longer, rushed to the altar to rouse her from prayer and seek her assurance... Lioba rose up from prayer and, as if she had been challenged to a contest, flung off the cloak which she was wearing and boldly opened the doors of the church. Standing on the threshold, she made a sign of the cross, opposing to the fury of the storm the name of the High God. Then she stretched out her hands towards heaven and three times invoked the mercy of Christ, praying that through the intercession of Holy Mary, the Virgin, He would quickly come to the help of His people. Suddenly God came to their aid. The sound of thunder died away, the winds changed direction and dispersed the heavy clouds, the darkness rolled back and the sun shone, bringing calm and peace. Thus did divine power make manifest the merits of His Handmaid. Unexpected peace came to His people and fear was banished."

Eventually Lioba occupied such a high position among the German missionaries that Saint Boniface gave her special honors:

"Sometimes she came to the Monastery of Fulda to say her prayers, a privilege never granted to any woman either before or since, because from the day that monks began to dwell there entrance was always forbidden to women. Permission was only granted to her, for the simple reason that the holy martyr Saint Boniface had commended her to the seniors of the monastery and because he had ordered her remains to be buried there....In spite of these special privileges, as a woman she was expected to follow special regulations: Her disciples and companions were left behind in a nearby cell and she entered the monastery always in daylight, with one nun older than the rest; and after she had finished her prayers and held a conversation with the brethren, she returned towards nightfall to her disciples whom she had left behind in the cell."

48

However, upon her death, the monks feared to carry out Saint Boniface's burial orders:

"...She died in the month of September. Her body, followed by a long cortege of noble persons, was carried by the monks of Fulda to their monastery with every mark of respect. Thus the seniors there remembered what Saint Boniface had said, namely, that it was his last wish that her remains should be placed next to his bones. But because they were afraid to open the tomb of the blessed martyr [Boniface] they discussed the matter and decided to bury her on the north side of the altar which the martyr Saint Boniface had himself erected and consecrated in honor of the Saviour and the twelve Apostles."[5]

Even after death various miracles were said to have occurred at her burial place when pilgrims asked for divine help.

Saint Lioba lived a long and active life in the 8th century. She organized convents for nuns in Germany, gave spirtual advice to Emperor Charlemagne and miracles were attributed to her both during and after her lifetime.

Saint Catherine of Siena

Catherine Benincasa—Saint Catherine of Siena—was in some ways a contrast to Saint Lioba, a woman of physical power. Although her influence was great, her physical body was frail—partly because of the life of denial she imposed upon herself.

Saint Catherine of Siena as depicted in a fresco by Antoniazzo Roma, now damaged by water.

Saint Catherine was born in the mid-14th century after Europe had been Christianized. Many problems still remained for the Church. This was a century of violent events such as famines, the plague of the Black Death, the beginning of the 100 Years War and rumored corruption within the Church. Yet at the time of Catherine's birth, the city-state of Siena in Italy was prosperous and

---

[5]Rudolf, Monk of Fulda, "The Life of Saint Leoba," C. H. Talbot, tr. *The Anglo-Saxon Missionaries in Germany,* (New York: Sheed and Ward, 1954), p. 210-224. Note that Talbot spells her name Leoba—the modern translation is Lioba. This spelling is used throughout.

beautiful. Her father, a wool dyer by trade, was not rich but comfortably well-off. Catherine's mother was in charge of their large and complex household. In all, she gave birth to 25 children, Catherine and a twin sister, Giovanna, being the next to last. Since Catherine's mother was only able to nurse one baby, Giovanna was given to a wet-nurse. This twin sister died in infancy as did the last baby, so Catherine became the youngest of this large family. She seems to have been her mother's favorite child.[6] Like Lioba, as a child Catherine was reported showing special piety. At six she was said to have received a vision of Christ blessing her; at seven she took a vow of chastity promising Christ to remain a virgin for her whole life. Her family, not knowing of this vow, engaged her to be married when she was 12. Catherine cut her hair and veiled her face to avoid appearing attractive to her suitor.

When she finally confessed her vow and revealed a determination not to marry, her family gave way. She became a Dominican Tercerary nun[7] but also chose to live as a recluse in a tiny room of the family home. Living a life of prayer, speaking only to her confessor/priest, she ate and drank little and is said to have disciplined her body to sleep less than an hour a night. After three years of this self-imposed isolation, she experienced a mystical union with Jesus and thereafter left isolation to do charitable work in the outside world.

While Lioba gained her reputation through teaching and spiritual leadership, Catherine gained a reputation for mystical experiences. After her return to the world she continued to experience these visions. Her behavior was sometimes considered strange, even frightening, but her trance-like ecstasies slowly gained her a reputation for holiness and a following of disciples. One of Catherine's biographers described these states of ecstasy from a quote by one of her followers:

"From the time when she began her life of active charity, her familiarity with the secrets of the supernatural world became more apparent to the world around her. When her soul rose upwards in prayer and contemplation, her body became as rigid, cold and insensible as a stone. It happened also that her companions saw the motionless, kneeling woman lifted from the floor 'so high that one could put one's hand between Catherine and the floor'—they had certainly tried for themselves. At other times, and especially after she had received the Body of the Lord in the Blessed Sacrament, as she lay withdrawn in ecstasy, it was as though her body were flooded with such heat that beads of sweat appeared all over her flushed face . . .

"Sometimes her ecstasies [during mass] lasted right up to midday when the church was closed for a couple of hours, as was the custom while the whole of Siena took its siesta. Then the church-wardens took the unconscious girl and carried her outside and let her lie in the street in front of the church door.

---

[6]Sigrid Undset, *Catherine of Siena* (London: Sheed and Ward, 1954), p. 15.

[7]As a Dominican Tercerary or Mantellate Catherine wore a black and white nun's habit. This order was made up of devout women who lived under religious rule in their own homes—not in convents.

Passers-by, and those who thought that over-zealous Christians and exaggeratedly pious women were a public nuisance, would give her a kick or slap as they went by. When Catherine wakened again she had to limp home covered with bruises and spattered with dirt from the street.

"But after a while the little flock who believed in Catherine's holiness grew. They gathered round this young woman who they loved because she was always patient, gay and smiling. . . . They asked her for advice whenever they had either spiritual or material difficulties. . ."[8]

As her reputation as a holy visionary grew, so did her group of devoted followers. Catherine began to exert a powerful influence on the affairs of her time.

Catherine negotiated tirelessly to get Pope Gregory XI to return to Rome from Avignon, France. She also urged him to make reforms within the Church. Pope Gregory was an admirable person but seems to have been attached both to his French homeland and to various unworthy members of his own family for whom he did unnecessary favors. In a series of letters, Catherine urged him to return to Rome. Here she felt that he, as Pope, could strengthen and reform the Church because the Vatican was the traditional center for the Roman Catholic faith. The following passages are taken from one of Catherine's many letters to Pope Gregory XI. This letter is representative of the correspondence that she carried on with Gregory over several years. As you read some of her correspondence consider these things about Saint Catherine:

- She was a dyer's daughter raised in a simple, hardworking family.
- She had not been taught to read or write—her followers wrote down her spoken words.[9]
- From age 17-20 she had lived in a small cell at her home in Siena, in isolation from the world.
- This correspondence with Pope Gregory was begun when she was 23 years old.
- She was one of an order of simple Dominican nuns and yet her letters were written to the Pope, the highest authority of the Roman Catholic Church.

In this passage Catherine begged Pope Gregory to rid the Church of corruption especially by the replacement of priests who seemed more interested in worldly goods than in living their vows of poverty:

"In the Name of Jesus Christ crucified and of sweet Mary: Most holy and dear and sweet father in Christ sweet Jesus: I your unworthy daughter Catherine, servant and slave of the servants of Jesus Christ, write to you. Therefore, I beg you, sweet my father, to use the instrument of your power and virtue, with zeal, and hungry desire for the peace and honor of God and this I tell

[8]Undset, *Catherine of Siena*, p. 58-60.

[9]Although she learned to read and write three years before her death, she seems to have continued to use secretaries for her numerous correspondence.

you, on behalf of Christ crucified, it befits you to achieve three chief things through your power. [Get rid of] the bad priests and rulers who poison and rot that garden. Ah me, you our Governor, do you use your power to pluck out those flowers! Throw them away, that they may have no rule! Insist that they study to rule themselves in holy and good life. Alas, what confusion is this, to see those who ought to be a mirror of voluntary poverty, appear in such luxury and state and pomp and worldly vanity.''[10]

Futher she told Gregory that he must return to Rome from Avignon, France and organize a crusade aimed at capturing the Holy Lands from the Turkish Muslims.

"I tell you, father in Christ Jesus, come swiftly [back to Rome] like a gentle lamb. Respond to the Holy Spirit who calls you. I tell you, Come, come, come, and do not wait for time since time does not wait for you....Raise the standard of the holy Cross; thus raising this standard, which seems to me the refreshment of Christians, we shall be freed—we from our wars and divisions and many sins, the infidel people from their infidelity. In this way you will come and attain the reformation, giving good priests to Holy Church....I say no more...''[11]

In 1377 Catherine's pleading finally helped convince Gregory to come to Rome. He died a year later. Urban VI, elected the next Pope, turned out to be harsh and unpopular—so much so that his election was declared invalid. Pope Clement VII was appointed in his place. Since England remained faithful to Urban—France and Naples to Clement—war raged between the divided groups. Catherine defended Urban and

helped to reconcile Rome to his rule. Catherine also carried on extensive correspondence with Queen Giovanna of Naples, negotiated peace settlements among several warring city-states and created a new monastery from a gift of a castle given to her by a devoted follower. Throughout her short life, another of Catherine's concerns were her charitable acts. The following excerpt shows something of this aspect of Catherine's life. It also demonstrates how Catherine's compassion included individuals caught in the politics of the time. This particular letter has been called "one of the famous letters of the world"[12] and has been translated into many languages. The letter was written to Catherine's friend and confessor, Brother Raimonda, recounting the execution of a young man on the charge of criticizing the government of Siena. The youth, Niccolo Tuldo, was in despair when Catherine went to comfort him and to help give meaning to his death. Here Catherine described his execution in her famous letter:

"I went to visit (Niccolo)...and he made me promise by the love of God that when the time of the sentence should come, I would be with him. So I promised, and did.

---

[10]There were several unsuccessful crusades in the 13th century—for example there was a "childrens' " crusade and the last crusade of this period was conducted by King Louis IX or France in 1270. He died during the crusade.

[11]Vida D. Scudder, tr., *Saint Catherine of Siena as Seen in Her Letters* (London: J. M. Dent, 1911), p. 131-133.

[12]*Ibid.*, p. 109.

Then in the morning, before the bell rang, I went to him: and he received great consolation. I led him to hear Mass, and he received the Holy Communion, which he had never before received. His will was accorded and submitted to the will of God; and only one fear was left, that of not being strong at the moment. But the measureless and glowing goodness of God deceived him, creating in him such affection and love in the desire of God that he did not know how to abide without Him, and said: 'Stay with me, and do not abandon me. So it shall not be otherwise than well with me. And I die content.' "[13]

In April, 1380, Saint Catherine died at 33 years of age. She had exhausted herself working to end the wars between Popes Urban and Clement and had lived a life of severe denial, particularly during her last months. Father Raimondo described eight miracles which happened to people who came to honor her as her body lay in state. It was reported that her body did not decompose before burial. Catherine died young after an ascetic life, possessing few personal belongings and existing on a near starvation diet. Yet she had worked actively for church reform, peace and charity. Her power, vitality and effectiveness seemed to have been based partly upon the awe in which medieval Christians held her. In a time filled with dreadful events such as the plague of the Black Death, famines, and wars, they fervently believed in her special holiness.

Saint Joan of Arc

Perhaps the most famous saint in history is Saint Joan of Arc. In many ways she stands outside the tradition of the saints previously described in these essays. Saint Lioba's sanctity was partly based on her activities in converting the pagans of Saxony. Saint Catherine's energies were often directed at being peacemaker to the warring factions in the Roman Catholic Church of her day. The next saint to be considered, Teresa, acted as a reformer within the Church as an answer to the Protestant Reformation. These women were primarily interested in a spiritual life devoted to their religious faith and the Church. All three were canonized within a century of their deaths. All three have left vivid impressions of mature, powerful, yet spiritual personalities.

In contrast, Joan's major task— her "divine mission"—seems to have had no obvious spiritual purpose. She felt that she had been commanded by God to lead a French army to raise the British siege of the French city of Orleans and to drive the British army from France. Her goal may seem patriotic, unrelated to religious aims. Saint Joan was not canonized by the Church until 1920—five hundred years after she lived. Joan's brief life leaves the impression of a young woman while the others leave that of fully developed adult personalities. Joan even called herself "Jeanne la Pucelle" or Joan the Maid. It is, then, as a determined yet innocent maid that history and literature has generally pictured Joan.

---

[13]*Ibid.*, p. 112.

Sketch of Joan of Arc done in 1429 perhaps is the only drawing of Joan done during her lifetime, the artist did it from his imagination as he had not actually met her.

Her life story is simple yet amazing. She was born in the small village of Domremy in Lorraine, France, in 1412. Her parents were farmer/peasants and devoted Roman Catholics. Until Joan was 17 she had traveled outside her village only twice. She had had no schooling and could neither read nor write.

In 1424, when Joan was 13, she suddenly heard a voice speaking that she believed was God. She reported that this happened several times a week until the Archangel Michael appeared to her and said:

"Joan, you are destined by Fate to lead a life very much different from what you are now living, and to accomplish miraculous things, for you have been chosen by the King of Heaven to restore the Kingdom of France, and to aid and protect King Charles. . . . You shall put on man's clothes, bear arms and become the head of the army."[14]

Other saints appeared before her and later she was instructed by them to go to the town of Chinon where the crown prince, Dauphin of France, resided. There she was to get the Dauphin's permission to lead a French army against the English siege of Orleans. After this she was told to crown the Dauphin as King Charles and drive the English out of France.

Joan kept her voices a secret for five years. Finally, she confided her secret to a relative who took her to the French general, Robert de Baudricourt. He immediately sent her home. In January, 1428, when the English began the siege at Orleans, Joan took this as a sign that it was time to act on the commands of her voices. Baudricourt was persuaded to help Joan and, as instructed, she journeyed to Chinon to speak to the Dauphin.

The Dauphin, suspicious of the authenticity of Joan's visions, set a trap for her. He had a nobleman sit in his own official chair and hid behind others at the back of the room. Joan entered and started toward the nobleman, then she stopped, walked through the crowd to the Dauphin. When she had fallen to her knees in front of him she spoke:

---

[14]Quoted in: Ingvald Raknem, *Joan of Arc in History, Legend and Literature* (Oslo, Norway: Universitetsforlaget, 1971), p. 10.

"Gentle Dauphin, my name is Joan the Maid. The King of Heaven sends me to you with the message that you shall be anointed and crowned in the city of Reims, and that you shall be the lieutenant of the King of Heaven, who is the King of France."[15]

The Dauphin was impressed that Joan had identified him in the crowd but still had doubts about her plans. After leaders debated and tested her plans they were accepted. She was given her own apartment at the castle so she could confer daily with the Dauphin. After further delays, she cut her hair, put on armor and male dress and led a relief force of about 4000 soldiers against the British siege.

Although the French army commanders had little faith in this girl's military ability, she greatly inspired the soldiers who followed her lead during the storming of the city walls. The British abandoned Orleans in a week. In a month Joan stood by the Dauphin as he was crowned King of France. Following the coronation, kneeling before him, she said:

"Gentle King, now is fulfilled the will of God that I should raise the siege of Orleans and lead you to the city of Reims to receive the holy coronation, to show you that you are indeed the king and the rightful lord of the realm of France."[16]

Other military successes followed the lifting of the siege. Joan seems to have had a "paralyzing effect on the English soldiers."[17] Consequently the British determined to defeat and capture her. At Compiegne she was captured by the pro-British Burgundians and after one abortive attempt to escape, she was ransomed to the British. Joan's five month trial that followed was conducted mostly by 164 pro-British clergy and Burgundians. King Charles did not try to rescue her. One of the major charges against her was that her voices were false and that her belief in them had led her into heresy. She was condemned to death and burned at the stake as a witch on May 30, 1428 at the town of Rouen. Joan was nineteen years old at her death.

This, briefly, was Joan of Arc's history. Her visions, her devotion to France, her trial and death at the stake have so captured the imaginations of individuals that one authority says that 12,000 works were published about her before 1920—and many more since her canonization.[18] With few exceptions (such as William Shakespeare's treatment of Joan as a witch in *Henry VI, Part I*), Joan has been depicted sympathetically and heroically. In the early 1800's Napoleon Bonaparte made Joan a symbol of French nationalism and she became an official French hero. Since her canonization in 1920, even more interest has surrounded her life and achievements. Her youth, visions, purity and innocence have appeared in vivid contrast to her masculine attire and military successes. Finally, her death at such a young age has created a tragic-romantic atmosphere that has made her story an irresistible subject for writers, filmmakers and historians.

---

[15]*Ibid.*, p. 12.

[16]*Ibid.*, p. 14

[17]*Ibid.*, p. 12.

[18]*Ibid.*, p. 1.

Saint Teresa in a mystical trance as depicted by the Italian sculptor, Lorenzo Bernini

Saint Teresa

Unlike Catherine and Joan of Arc Teresa was born in 1515 into a wealthy noble family. She was described as beautiful and intelligent. Perhaps because of these attributes, following her mother's death her father placed her in the care of nuns to protect her from becoming too worldly. While living in the convent, Teresa determined to live a religious life and joined an order of Carmelite nuns. As had become common in the 15th and 16th centuries, this order did not follow a particularly strict rule. The nuns were allowed visitors—both male and female. Meditation and prayer were difficult in the free and over-crowded atmosphere of the convent.[19] For eighteen years in the convent, Teresa fought what she saw as her own pleasure loving nature while she searched for spiritual fulfillment. Later she wrote

about the convent—*"the road to religion is so little traveled that a nun who wishes to follow it has more to fear from her companions than all the devils."*[20]

At 40 she finally overcame the temptations of the world and began a new life of mystical contemplation. When she was 45, Teresa founded a reformed convent of strict Carmelite rule. The plan was for a small group of nuns to live in simplicity and poverty, in isolation from the world. One of Saint Teresa's biographers described their life in the enclosed convent in the following way:

"The house was small, with a small but neat chapel: there was neither a common workroom nor a common dormitory. Little shelters were erected in the garden for meditation. The day was portioned out between work and prayer. The nuns rose at six; until eight in summer and nine in winter they were occupied in prayer...As to the hour of the meal it was unsettled, as it depended on whether there was anything to eat. The food of the nuns, if they were not reduced to dry bread only, consisted of a little coarse fish or bread and cheese. During the time of recreation which followed they might converse with each other as they pleased; then the convent was buried in silence while some slept and some prayed....The

---

[19]Ethel Rolt-Wheeler, *Women of the Cell and Cloister* (London: Methuen & Co., 1913), p. 231-232.

[20]Quoted in *Ibid.*, p. 232.

nuns habits were of black serge with a cape and scapulary of white woolen serge; the coifs were of coarse flax cloth, the tunics of woolen serge; on their feet the nuns wore hemp-soled sandals."[21]

After five years of enclosed life, Teresa was called to organize other Carmelite monasteries of primitive rule by the local bishop. In the 15 years that remained of her life, she founded 30 new monasteries for women and two for men.[22] This required constant traveling throughout Spain over terrible roads. It also meant trying to live a pious life under harsh physical surroundings. In her autobiography Teresa, then 50 years old, described some of the trials she and her companions suffered during their travels:

Teresa commented on a journey to Burgos in southern Spain:

"We could not find any way of going on, for there was water everywhere, and on either side it was very deep. . . . If the carriages heeled slightly, all would be lost. . . . When I saw that we were entering a world of water, with no sign of a path or a boat, even I was not without fear."

One of her companions, another nun, also described this incident:

"Once when we were going along a river bank, the mud was so thick that the carriages stuck in it and we had to get down. After escaping from this danger we were climbing a hill when we espied before our eyes another and a worse one. For the holy Mother saw the carriage in which her nuns were traveling about to overturn, and the hill we were climbing was so steep that even a large number of people could not have saved them by preventing the carriage from falling. But at the same moment one of the youths whom we had with us saw

it and seized the wheel and saved the carriage from overturning."

Often their carriage became like a furnace in the heat of Spain:

"We went under a bridge to have our siesta, so that we could get a little shade. There were some pigs there, but we drove them away and took their places; and so fierce was the sun that we thought ourselves very lucky to have [some shade]."

Decent lodgings were impossible to find. Teresa had become ill and was running a fever. Her companion, Maria de San Jose described the room in an inn where the nuns took her for shelter:

". . . I think there had been pigs [in the room]. The ceiling was so low that we could hardly stand upright, the sun came in on all sides and the place was full of cobwebs and infested with vermin. . . "[23]

Even with all these problems, there was a growing recognition of the value of Teresa's work. People came out to greet them as they passed. Once even a triumphal march of villagers accompanied them to the next town.[24] Through her leadership new monasteries were founded. During these journeys Teresa suffered because of the conditions of travel in 16th century Spain, but she also kept to her strict regimen or rule. On occasions,

---

[21] *Ibid.*, p. 254.

[22] *Ibid.*, p. 256.

[23] E. Allison Peers, *Saint Teresa of Jesus* (London: Faber and Faber, 1953), p. 25-29.

[24] *Ibid.*, p. 29.

beginning in 1556, Teresa experienced states of mystical ecstasy—and visions similar to those of Catherine of Siena. She described her first experience which involved hearing voices:

"One day, having prayed for some time, I began the hymn; and as I was saying it, I fell into a trance—so suddenly, that I was, as it were, carried out of myself. I have no doubt about it, for it was most plain.

This was the first time that our Lord bestowed on me the grace of ecstasy. I heard these words: 'I will not have thee converse with men, but with angels.' This made me wonder very much. They made me afraid,—though, on the other hand, they gave me great comfort, which, when I had lost the fear, remained with me."[25]

She described trances many times:

"It please the Lord that I should sometimes see the following vision. I would see beside me, on my left hand, an angel in bodily form—a type of vision which I am not in the habit of seeing, except very rarely. Though I often see representations of angels, my visions of them are of the type which I first mentioned. It pleased the Lord that I should see this angel in the following way. He was not tall, but short, and very beautiful, his face so aflame that he appeared to be one of the highest types of angel who seem to be all afire."[26]

As these ecstasies and visions became known, the Spanish Inquisition became suspicious that Teresa might be faking these visions. The Inquisition investigated persons suspected of witchcraft and heresy. This instrument of the Catholic Church had become extremely powerful and was greatly

feared in 16th century Spain. Teresa's autobiography was sent for examination to the Holy Office of the Inquisition at Madrid and she never saw it again. In 1586, four years after Teresa's death, the Inquisition finally approved the book and released it to a follower of Teresa's Anne of Jesus, who had it published.[27]

Though the Inquisition was at times suspicious of her, Teresa saw herself as a defender of the Church. She was born two years before Martin Luther posted his Ninety-Five Theses on the church door at Wittenberg which inaugurated the Protestant Reformation. As a committed Roman Catholic, Teresa imagined Luther as the devil incarnate and envisioned converts to Lutheranism as heretics. She described one experience of hell in her life:

"It was that vision that filled me with the very great distress which I feel at the sight of so many lost souls, especially of the Lutherans,—for they were once members of the Church by baptism,—and also gave me the most vehement desires for the salvation of souls; for certainly I believe that, to save even one from those overwhelming torments, I would most willingly endure many deaths . . . and I know not how we can be calm, when we see Satan carry so many souls daily away."[28]

---

[25]David Lewis, tr., *The Life of St. Teresa of Jesus* (London: St. Anselm's Society, 1888), p. 187.

[26]Robert T. Petersson, *The Art of Ecstasy, Teresa, Bernini and Cranshaw* (New York: Atheneum, 1970), p. 40.

[27]Lewis, tr., *The Life*, Preface: xvii-xviii.

[28]*Ibid.*, p. 264-265.

Although Teresa believed strongly that those who left the Catholic faith were sinners, she also recognized a need to reform the Spanish monastery system. Her founding of simple Carmelite monasteries was meant to return religious life to what she believed should be its central purposes: simplicity, devotion to prayer and meditation. Teresa witnessed a decline in religious orders; in the 14th-15th centuries the high level of scholarship of European monasteries had all but disappeared. Saint Teresa helped bring about a rebirth of scholarship through books written by her on the spiritual life as well as by her autobiography. One modern scholar has called her "Possibly. . .the first modern woman to become an eminent writer."[29]

Monasteries founded by her on strict rules of poverty and prayer helped return the Spanish Catholic Church of her time to more spiritual goals. Teresa died in 1582 at the age of 67.

Teresa can therefore be seen as central to the Roman Catholic Counter-Reformation which worked to stop Luther and other dissenters, yet reformed the Roman Catholic Church. Finally, her Carmelite convents spread throughout Roman Catholic Europe and offered a refuge for women who wished to live a strict spiritual life. Two hundred years after Teresa's death, a Carmelite convent became the sanctuary of one unusual woman. After a life at court as mistress of King Louis XIV of France, Louise, Duchesse of de La Valla, left this life and became a nun. A Carmelite convent gave Louise the chance to do penance and achieve spiritual peace after a worldly life. Thus, the orders that Saint Teresa started continued to provide options for women of many situations and classes.

★ ★ ★ ★ ★ ★

During medieval times in Europe, the Church offered some women a chance to achieve leadership positions. As missionaries, reformers, mediators in political disputes and even, like Saint Joan, as military leaders, these saintly women influenced events of their time in ways not normally available to ordinary medieval women.

Points to Consider

1. Reviewing the saints' lives: For each or the four women saints described here jot down the following information:

   The century in which they lived.

   Their childhood—Where it was spent. What is known about it?

   The length of their lives.

   Their main spiritual/religious activities.

   Their major worldly activities or contributions to political life.

2. Saint Lioba

   How would you describe Saint Lioba?

   What kind of miraculous accomplishments were attributed to her?

   Why do you think the monks did not carry out Saint Boniface's order to bury Lioba by him?

   Why do you think Lioba was made a saint?

---

[29]Petersson, *The Art of Ecstasy*, p. 14.

3. Saint Catherine of Siena

How might Catherine's childhood have made her desire a religious life of self-denial?

Why do you think this illiterate and simple woman came to have such a strong influence on Popes and rulers?

Why do you think the Roman Catholic Church saw Catherine worthy of sainthood?

4. Saint Joan of Arc

What specific aspects of Joan's life and mission seem different than those of these other saints?

In what ways was her life similar to other saints' lives discussed here?

Why do you think Joan was seen worthy of sainthood? Why do you think the Roman Catholic Church took so long to decide to canonize her?

What similarities do you notice in the lives of these saints?

What differences?

5. Saint Teresa of Avila

What do you think was Teresa's major accomplishment?

How can Teresa be viewed as part of the Catholic Counter-Reformation which aimed to reform the Roman Catholic Church and contain Protestantism?

Why do you think the Roman Catholic Church saw Teresa worthy of sainthood?

GROUP DISCUSSION

Medieval and Renaissance times saw hundreds of people canonized as saints. Only four of these women saints have been discussed here. Below are four more sketches of important or representative medieval saints. As a group activity read over all eight and discuss:

What characteristics do they seem to have in common?

What characteristics are different?

How do their roles seem different from those that most medieval women were expected to perform?

Why do you believe that these women were seen as particularly holy or saint-like?

Notice where all these saints were born. What might this suggest about roles for women within the Roman Catholic Church?

Which of these women would you most admire? Why?

Saints Marana and Cyra:

They were 3rd century ascetic recluses who lived for 40 years in a "mandra"—a space surrounded by a wall but open to the sky. They are said to have worn heavy chains around their necks, waists and feet. They were covered with veils and spent all their time in prayer. They depended entirely upon the charity of people outside their walls to provide them with food and water. They lived this severely restricted life so that they could focus all their thoughts on God.[30]

---

[30]Ethel Rolt-Wheeler, *Women of the Cell and Cloister* (London: Methuen & Co., 1913), p. 12-13.

Saint Mary of Egypt

A 4th century ascetic of the early church, she had lived a wanton life of luxury in Alexandria, Egypt. Upon her conversion to Christianity, she went to live alone in a cave in the desert to do penance for her evil past. There she lived for forty-seven years in complete solitude except for two brief encounters with a monk, Zosimus, to whom she told her history.[31]

Saint Brigid of Ireland

(c. 453-525) A 5th century nun and abbess, she gained many followers and founded a religious order. Many miracles are attributed to Saint Brigid. She is supposed to have cured the sick and insane. Her symbol was milk—and it was said that her special qualities were those of a loving mother.[32]

Saint Bridget of Sweden:

(1303-1373) Contemporary of Saint Catherine of Siena, Saint Bridget was married and had eight children. However, even as a child, Bridget experienced visions and mystical experiences that continued into her adult life. Finally, she and her husband renounced the world and entered a convent. In 1349, after the death of her husband, she went to Rome and remained there except for one journey to the Holy Land. She helped Saint Catherine of Siena persuade the Pope to return to Rome from Avignon. She founded convents of Brigittines based on her rule. Her mystical visions were written down by her biographers.

[31] *Ibid.*, p. 17-21.

[32] *Ibid.*, p. 35-38. One recent scholar also connects St. Brigid with a pre-Christian Celtic female God, Brigit. He thinks the milk symbol and Brigit were part of pastoral festivals with ewes coming into milk in the spring. See: Peter Berresford Ellis, *Caesar's Invasion of Britain.* (New York: New York University Press, 1978), p. 32-34.

C. Women and the Protestant Reformation
Reformers and Followers

The Reformation can be seen as a double reform movement. There was one reform movement which ultimately led Martin Luther, John Calvin and others to break with the Roman Catholic Church and form new Protestant congregations. There was another reform movement within the Roman Catholic Church which aimed at ridding the Church of corruption, stricter rule for monasteries and the quieting of dissent by way of investigations done by the Inquisition. Both of these Reformations effected changes for women although neither had women's concerns as a primary goal.

From the early beginnings of the Reformation, women had prominent roles on both sides of the conflicts. The following descriptions are only meant to suggest a few Reformation women's activities and some of the differences between the various reformers. These selected sketches cannot fully serve to indicate the great numbers of women involved in these reforms and the extent of their contributions both as leaders and as followers.

Women Who Aimed At Reforming the Roman Catholic Church From Within

St. Catherine of Siena and St. Teresa of Avila

The two most famous of the Roman Catholic women reformers who led reform movements within the Roman Catholic Church have already been discussed in this book. These are St. Catherine of Siena (1347-1380), one of the early reformers, and St. Teresa of Avila, a reformer of the Counter-Reformation of the 16th century. Although from different time periods with different aims, both women were:

- spiritually committed and they testified to having had mystical experiences in their autobiographies.
- unafraid of challenging important men of the Catholic hierarchy (Priests, Bishops and Popes) if they felt they were wrong or corrupt.
- surrounded by large numbers of followers—both men and women—who believed in their special sanctity.
- suspected by other groups of having false mystical experiences, St. Teresa was even investigated by the Inquisition.
- influential in reforms made within the Church. St. Catherine influenced the Pope to return to Rome, St. Teresa founded the stricter rule of the Carmelite Order of nuns that spread in Europe and the Americas after the 16th century.

Katherine Von Bora

Angela Merici, Mary Ward and Louise de Marillac

There were other important women reformers within the Roman Catholic Church. In the 15th and 16th centuries Angela Merici, Mary Ward and Louise de Marillac founded three new orders of nuns (Ursulines, Institute of the Blessed Virgin Mary and the Daughters of Charity) which provided alternatives to the enclosed convents being organized by the Roman Catholic Church during the Counter Reformation.[1] These orders emphasized simple vows (less severe and binding) and dedication to the Church while requiring nuns to carry on works of charity in the outside world.[2]

Reformation women who broke away from the Catholic Church and helped to form Protestant Congregations

Katherine von Bora (1499-1550)

Several women of the reformation became prominent as part of husband and wife teams—both being reformers. Katherine von Bora was a nun who left the convent on the advice of Martin Luther and

[1]Ruth P. Liebowitz, "Virgins in the Service of Christ: The Dispute Over an Active Apostolate for Women During the Counter-Reformation," in Rosemary Ruether and Eleanor McLaughlin, *Women of Spirit* (New York: Simon and Schuster), p. 132-133.

[2]*Ibid.*, p. 134-135.

eventually married him. Katherine endured attacks on her character because of her marriage. Martin also warned her that if he were burned at the stake she would also suffer this fate.[3] Katherine brought order to Martin's often chaotic life. She excelled as a medical practitioner; her son, who became a famous doctor called her a *"half doctor."*[4] She was particularly skilled in organizing the huge Luther household which included their six children, orphaned nephews and nieces as well as other relatives and theological students.

Katherine Zell (1497-1562)

Katherine Zell married a priest/reformer named Matthew Zell and they became, as one historian noted, a complete team.[5] Partly because both of their children died as infants, Katherine was able to devote all her energies to their reform activities. She organized relief for refugees during the Peasant War of 1525, she visited people in prison, whether she approved of their ideas or not. She preached and conducted a friend's funeral service. By leading religious services as a minister— thereby acting as a priest—she was said to be a *"disturber of the peace of the Church."*[6] She outlived her husband and continued with religious work until her death.

Wilbrandis Rosenblatt (1504-1564)

Wilbrandis Rosenblatt's contribution to the Reformation can be seen as mainly domestic but the families she organized and supported in the cause of reform might have undone a lesser woman. Wilbrandis was married four times and three of her husbands were Reformation leaders. She bore eleven children, nursed family members during an epidemic of the plague and followed her last husband, Martin Butzer, to England to live, leaving her home in Strasbourg, Germany. An Italian refugee who stayed with Wilbrandis and Martin before they left for England described their home:

"For 17 days after my arrival I was entertained in Butzer's home. It is like a hostel, receiving refugees for the cause of Christ. In his family during the entire time I saw not the least occasion of offense but only ground for edification. His table is not lavish nor sparse, but marked by a godly frugality."[7]

Considering that refugees were added to a household that already included many of their children and various relatives, the support Wilbrandis gave to her reformer-husbands was heroic.

Jeanne d'Albret

Katherine von Bora and Wilbrandis Rosenblatt were best known as reformers who were part of husband-wife teams. Jeanne d'Albret was a Protestant who was separated from her beloved husband by their religious differences.

Jeanne d'Albret was the only daughter of the "Margaret of Margarets" of Navarre; Jeanne

---

[3]Roland Bainton, *Women of the Reformation in Germany and Italy* (Boston: Beacon Press, 1971), p. 27.

[4]*Ibid.*, p. 29.

[5]*Ibid.*, p. 57.

[6]*Ibid.*, p. 72.

[7]*Ibid.*, p. 88.

Jeanne d'Albret

Jeanne d'Albret—Musee Conde, Chantilly. Giraudon photograph

came to be a strong follower of John Calvin and in 1560 she publicly announced her conversion to his Reform Protestant Church. She kept to her new faith (French Protestants were called Huguenots) even when her husband, Antoine de Bourbon, abandoned Calvinism to rejoin the Catholic Church. Jeanne said that by giving up the new Reform Church, Antoine had *"planted a thorn not in my foot, but in my heart"*[8]

Jeanne continued to support her new religion, even when the Huguenots were persecuted. Her husband threatened her with divorce and kept her under house arrest in the hope of forcing her to abandon her new faith. After being released, Jeanne left Antoine and made her way to Bearn, an area of southern France that she controlled as she did Navarre. Her husband was wounded in one of the wars of religion that plagued France. Jeanne immediately journeyed to Antoine to act as his nurse in his final hours and he again changed his religious views and professed to being a

Huguenot. Jeanne returned to Navarre on the Spanish border. She encouraged religious toleration in the areas under her control. In 1564, gravely ill with tuberculosis, Jeanne issued an edict (a binding statement by a ruler) on religious liberty. When riots or revolts occurred in her territories over religion, her policy was to suppress the violence and then issue a general amnesty. Finally, at La Rochelle she acted as queen-regent for her son Henry. She took part in organizing the Reform Church and in the religious wars that continued to rage around La Rochelle. In August 1571 the wars ended—for a time. Jeanne d'Albret died in 1572, before the massacre of St. Bartholomew rekindled religious warfare. She is said to have been the only 16th century ruler who put no one to death for religious reasons.[9]

Elizabeth Dirks (16th century)

Not all women of the Reformation acted as part of wife-husband teams. Elizabeth Dirks was a member of the Anabaptists. This was considered a radical reformation sect and Anabaptists were universally persecuted. Elizabeth was arrested in Holland which was under Catholic control. She refused to take an oath and was examined at length. When she refused to give the names of other Anabaptists or deny her faith, she was tortured:

---

[8]Quoted in Roland H. Bainton, *Women of the Reformation in France and England* (Boston: Beacon Press, 1975) (1973), p. 50.

[9]*Ibid.*, p. 62.

"Then they took her again before the council and brought her to the torture room. Hans, the executioner, was there. The Lords said, 'So far we have treated you gently. Since you won't confess we will put you to the torture.' The Procurator General said, 'Mr. Hans, take hold of her.' Mr. Hans answered, 'Oh, no, my Lords, she will confess voluntarily.' But since she would not, he put screws on her thumbs and on two forefingers till the blood spurted from the nails.

EXAMINERS: Confess and we will ease your pain. We told you to confess and not to call upon the Lord, your God!

But she held steadfastly to the Lord, her God, as above related. Then they eased her pain and she said, 'Ask me. I will answer, for I feel no pain any more at all as I did.'

EXAMINERS: Then won't you confess?

ELIZABETH: No, my Lords."[10]

Margaret Fell (1614-1702)

In the mid-1600's a new Protestant sect, Society of Friends, more commonly known as Quakers,[11] was founded by an English visionary, George Fox. Among his early followers was Margaret Fell, then married to a wealthy judge. After Judge Fell's death, Margaret Fell eventually married George Fox and her estate of Swarthmore, became *"the heart of the [Quaker] movement."*[12] She even wrote an appeal to Charles II on behalf of all Friends or Quakers. A basic belief of the Friends was that all people were blessed equally with what they called the inner light or God's spirit. Following this philosophy, in 1666 Margaret Fell published a sermon, "Women's Speaking Justified,

Proved and Allowed of by the Scriptures," that argued that women had an right equal with men to preach and a right for a full religious life.[13] Therefore, the Friends represented a sect that encouraged the full participation of women, both as believers and ministers. Women were seen as equals to men in religious matters, able to express all kinds of religious ideas.

Thus, Margaret Fell was a founder of the Society of Friends that, although a comparatively small group, would continue to have influence on the status of women.[14] Her activities in helping to found the Society of Friends might be viewed as ending the Reformation period.

Some women, then, who chose Protestantism and left the Roman Catholic Church tried new roles as religious ministers and thinkers. Other women who remained in the Roman Catholic Church went back to earlier traditions of strict piety or service. On both sides of the controversies there were strong, active women who contributed to religious changes of the Reformation era.

---

[10]Bainton, *Women of the Reformation in Germany and Italy*, p. 148.

[11]The term Quaker, though at first used mockingly, came to be commonly used by outsiders to the faith. Those within the faith continue to use Society of Friends and it is a practicing denomination today.

[12]Doris Mary Stenton, *The English Woman in History* (New York: Schocken Books, 1977)(1957), p. 177.

[13]*Ibid.*, p. 179.

[14]In United States history, reformers such as Lucretia Mott, Angelina and Sarah Grimke and Susan B. Anthony were Quakers.

POINTS TO CONSIDER

1. What seem to have been some of the characteristics that prominent Reformation women like Katherine von Bora, Katherine Zell and Wilbrandis Rosenblatt had in common?

   What do you think their major contributions were to the Protestant Reformation?

2. In what specific ways does Jeanne d'Albret differ from Katherine von Bora, Katherine Zell and Wilbrandis Rosenblatt?

   In what ways can Jeanne be looked at as an outstanding Protestant ruler?

3. Who was Elizabeth Dirks?

   Why was she tortured?

   Did she give in to torture?

4. Who was Margaret Fell?

   Why might she be seen as marking the end of the Reformation era?

5. Quakers represent a very small religious group. The influence of Quakers on rights for women (both religious and civil) has been much greater than their numbers.

   The following are excerpts from a letter of George Fox written when he was traveling and doing missionary work in North America. The letter was written to Quakers in England in the year 1672. As you read it over, note down on a piece of paper things that you notice about Fox's attitude toward women's roles in the Quaker religion:

   "Friends   1672
   Keep your women's meetings in the power of God...For man and woman were helps meet in the image of God, and in righteousness and holiness, in the dominion before they fell; but after the fall, in the transgression, the man was to rule over his wife; but in the restoration by Christ, into the image of God, and his righteousness and holiness again, in that they are helps meet, man and woman, as they were before the fall. Sarah obeyed Abraham, and called him lord. Abraham did also obey the voice of his wife Sarah, in casting out the bondwoman and her son. Dorcas, a woman, was a disciple. So there was a woman disciple, as well as men disciples; and mind the women that accompanied her. And women are to take up the cross daily, and follow Christ daily, as well as the men;....And there were elder women in the Truth as well as elder men in the Truth; so they have an office as well as the men,...

   "Deborah was a judge; Miriam and Huldah were prophetesses; old Anna was a prophetess, and a preacher of Christ, to all them that looked for redemption in Jerusalem. Mary Magdalen, and the other Mary, were the first preachers of Christ's resurrection to the disciples, and the disciples could not believe their message and testimony that they had from Jesus, as some now a days cannot; but they received the command, and being sent preached it. So is every woman and man to do,...daughters shall prophesy as well as sons....Women are to prophesy; and prophecy is not to be quenched. They that have the testimony of Jesus are commanded to keep it, whether men or women....So in the church there were women

instructors, and prophetesses, and daughters prophetesses in the church; for Philip had four virgins that were prophetesses; and there were women disciples in the church, and women elders in the church, as well as men. So women are to keep in the government of Christ, and to be obeyers of Christ;... And the elder women in the Truth were not only called elders, but mothers....So the elder women and mothers are to be teachers of good things, and to be teachers of the younger and trainers up of them in virtue, in holiness, in godliness and righteousness, in wisdom, and in the fear of the Lord, in the church of Christ. And if the unbelieving husband is sanctified by the believing wife, then who is the speaker, and who is the hearer? Surely such a woman is permitted to speak, and to work the works of God, and to make a member in the church; and then as an elder, to oversee that they walk according to the order of the gospel. G.F.''[15]

What specific reasons does George Fox give for believing that Quaker women should be religious ministers and teachers like men?

Why do you think so many women leaders in women's rights movements have been Quakers?

In what ways does George Fox deserve to be called a male feminist (defender of women's rights)?

6. What reforms did women help to make within the Roman Catholic Church as part of the Counter-Reformation?

How might convent reforms of St. Teresa in Spain be contrasted with those convent reforms of Angela Merici, Mary Ward and Louise de Marillac?

7. Historians have debated whether the Protestant Reformation brought positive, negative or little change in the status of women. The Reformation did eventually mean that people dissatisfied with one sect or church could leave to find (or found) another. Sometimes they were persecuted, had to flee their own countries and even go to the New World but, at least, it might be possible to hold a new faith. Why might the fact that there were various choices of religious groups have helped women to gain more rights within the various Protestant sects?

GROUP EXERCISE:

Was There A Reformation for Women?

There were women within the Roman Catholic Church who worked for reform. There were women who left the Church and joined Protestant groups. Both groups worked for changes that they saw as beneficial to Christian believers. Historians are still debating, however, the question of whether the Protestant Reformation was beneficial to the status of women. In other words, did women gain or lose through the

---

[15]Samuel Tuke, ed., *The Epistles of George Fox* (New England: Obadiah Brown's Benevolent Fund, 1879), p. 144-146.

69

changes brought about by the Protestant Reformation? The following is a list of some of the changes that occurred during the Reformation that particularly affected the status and roles of women. After looking over the list, decide whether you think each change positively helped, left unchanged or had a negative effect on womens' status.

1. The idea of a "**Priesthood of all Believers**" was advocated by Martin Luther and other Protestants. Each member of the congregation was charged with teaching and praying for each other. As Luther explained it was, *"to do all those things which we see performed...by...the office of priest."*[16]

2. Married life was superior to a life of celibacy. Again as Luther put it, *"The married state is not only equal to all other states but preeminent [superior] over them all..."*[17]

3. The family was considered to be *"the school of faith"* where people learn to live as Christians while dealing with worldly problems and where even domestic chores are *"golden, noble works."*[18]

4. There was a shift to companion marriage where sexual union was seen as good and husband and wife were to be friendly helpmates. Marriage was not solely focused on procreation (having children) and a sexual double standard was not permitted.

5. The Virgin Mary was considered less important by Protestants — the cult of the Virgin Mary and her worship by Roman Catholics was discredited.

6. Eve was considered less evil. As Martin Luther put it, *"The glory of motherhood was left to Eve."*

7. Convents (and the office of nun) were abolished by most Protestants.

8. Most Protestants believed that marriage was a woman's rightful state and she was to be obedient to her husband. The family continued to be patriarchal, wives were subject to their husbands and husbands were heads of the household.

9. Protestants felt that all Christians should be literate and public education was encouraged. Everyone should be able to read the Bible and Christian literature.

10. Most Protestant sects did not allow women as pastors or ministers. Even though women could teach themselves and their children about religion, most Protestants did not encourage women to preach in public.

- Add up what your group considers to be positive, unchanged or negative results for women from the Protestant Reformation.

- Compare your answers in class discussion with other groups.

- In what ways was there a Reformation for women? In what ways not?

---

[16]Quoted in, Jane Dempsey Douglass, "Women and the Continental Reformation," in *Religion and Sexism,* Rosemary Radford Reuther, ed., (New York: Simon and Schuster, 1974), p. 296.

[17]*Ibid.*, p. 295.

[18]*Ibid.*, p. 294-295.

Chapter 3
Economics and Women in
Medieval/Renaissance
Europe

A. Women's Property Rights
An Overview

No historian has yet tackled a book summarizing women's property rights in the medieval and Renaissance periods. Each area of Europe had different laws and customs about women's rights to property. For example, in early Irish society there were three types of marriages, depending on whether the woman or man brought property into that marriage.

- lanamnas camthincuir—both bring property and both get back their share in case of divorce.

- lanamnas forferthinchur—the goods were provided by the man but the woman had a right to household property in case of divorce.

- lanamannas for bantinchur—the goods were primarily brought by the woman, and the husband had only marginal rights in case of divorce, perhaps a fee for helping administer the property.[1]

Women of the Italian city-state of Venice had only one tradition of marriage, with the husband managing the joint goods brought by both. But Venetian women did control some parts of their own dowry money. Their wills illustrate a strong inclination to bring money back to their natal (birth) family and to help their female relatives with gifts of money.[2] In 13th century England it seems that the husband had control over his wife's dowry, especially when it was in the form of land. However,

---

[1]Donncha O'Corrain, "Women in Early Irish Society," in *Women in Irish Society in Historical Dimension,* Margaret MacCurtain and Donncha O'Corrain, eds., (Westport: Greenwood Press, 1979), p. 2-4.

[2]Stanley Chojnacki, "Patrician Women in Early Renaissance Venice," *Studies in the Renaissance,* Vol. 21 (1974), p. 199.

while a man could lease these dowry lands or rent them, he could not sell them without his wife's agreement.[3] In these three examples wives could

- control all of their goods brought to the marriage
- control most of the goods
- only have a final say in selling the property

Despite all these differences, a few generalizations might be made that reflect European customs.These have to do with rights of women who remained single or carried on a trade (a femmes soles), who married (femmes couvertes) and who became widows (dower rights).

If a woman remained single, she was usually regarded as *a femme sole* who controlled her own property and had the right to buy and sell this property as she wished. However, there were many forces operating against a woman remaining single. If she were an heiress, she was likely to be the ward of someone who would make sure she married. For example, the English heiress Catherine Willoughby, had her wardship bought by Lord Suffolk. He then married her at the age of 40 when she was just 12. Not surprisingly, Catherine later refused to force her own sons into marriage and said, *"It is wicked not to let children choose their own partners."*[4] In France, Louis XIV spared his cousin Anne Marie de Montpensier the trauma of a similar forced marriage. She personally supervised and, controlled her vast properties and went over the accounts with her bailiff. One of her bailiffs criticized her interest and said that it was not ladylike and that she knew too much about her own affairs.[5] Perhaps the reason Louis XIV did not force a marriage upon his ward was that he knew his sons would inherit her money eventually. However, Anne Marie de Montpensier was an exception because most women of wealth married. Marriage was the accepted social ideal of men and women who did not take vows of celibacy to enter monasteries or convents. Most heirs—both young men and women—were the wards of powerful kings or nobles. Therefore, it is not surprising that the majority of women did marry but that many had misgivings about their guardian's choice of marriage partner. Recent scholarship suggests that both female and male heirs could usually pay off their guardian with a kind of marriage tax so that they could marry someone of their own choosing.[6] Yet, if current scholarship is correct that ten percent of northern European women at the time never married, perhaps there were more *femmes soles* supporting themselves than are usually recognized.[7]

---

[3]Alan Macfarlane, *The Origins of English Individualism* (New York: Cambridge University Press, 1978), p. 115.

[4]Evelyn Read, *Catherine: Duchess of Suffolk* (London: Jonathan Cape, 1962), p. 67-77.

[5]Victoria Sackville-West, *Daughter of France: The Life of Anne Marie Louise d'Orleans de Montpensier* (London: Michael Joseph, 1959), p. 190.

[6]Sue Sheridan Walker "Free Consent and Marriage of Feudal Wards in Medieval England," *Journal of Medieval History,* Vol. 8, No. 2 (June, 1982), p. 124.

[7]Macfarlane, p. 160.

The term *femmes soles* was also used in another way. In the medieval period women were part of economic guilds and involved in many trades. Single women were, or course, *femmes soles* and responsible for their own earnings and debts. Especially in England, common law was modified to include married women as *femmes soles* if they were carrying on trade. This change may have been created to prevent husbands from being responsible for their wives' debts. Nevertheless, it gave married women a chance to be wealthy in their own right.[8]

Married women (*femmes couvertes*) generally had their own property controlled by their husbands and had little say over the property that their husbands brought to the marriage. By the use of marriage contracts, however, some provision might be made for allowances to wives or for particular household expenses. Husbands were expected to pay for the wives' expenses and were responsible for any debts they might incur. In the case of divorce (which was discouraged by the Church but did occur) the wife was entitled to her *dower* back.[9] Sometimes this created an international crisis. For example, Louis XI married Eleanor of France who brought the province of Aquitaine as her dowry. France, therefore, controlled this major province. But Eleanor, who was a forceful woman, did not get along with the more pious, quiet Louis. They had two daughters but no sons. Louis, desperate for a male heir, (French women could not inherit the throne) divorced Eleanor, thereby France lost Aquitaine. She then returned to Aquitaine and married the King of England. Louis found himself with the English on both sides of his boundaries. The example of Louis is extreme, but husbands frequently paled at the thought of what divorce might do to their finances and power if their wives dowries were lost from their control.

If a husband died before the wife, she became a widow and came into dower rights. Generally this meant that she inherited one-third of all the property, the rest going to other heirs, or to the eldest male. This dower land and property was to be the widow's support during her old age; often she had only a life interest to it and could not sell it. Upon her marriage or death, it went to the eldest male heir or, if there were none, to a female heir.[10] Wills could give widows rights to additional property and some widows became enormously rich by successive marriages, like Bess Hardwick of England.

A very wealthy widow might be vulnerable to a male ruler's attentions. King John of England forced widows under his control to pay heavily for the privilege of remaining single and avoid being forced by him to marry unsavory characters.[11] One of the measures of the famous Magna Carta was meant to remove that abuse from King John's power. In the stormy days of the medieval period, widows, like other heirs—both male and female—had to worry about being kidnapped and forced into marriage.

---

[8]Eileen Power, *Medieval Women* (London: Cambridge University Press, 1975), p. 10.

[9]Dower rights were property lands, goods or money which the bride's family gave to the marriage for her support.

[10]Frances and Joseph Gies, *Women in the Middle Ages* (New York: Barnes and Noble, 1978), p. 31.

[11]*Ibid.*, p. 28.

For example, several enterprising noblemen tried to capture Eleanor, the former French queen, on her way back to Aquitaine. It is no wonder that so many widows in early medieval days retired to the comparative safety of a convent under the protection of the Church. Legal cases brought against a widow's estate might also be hazardous to her security. Christine de Pisan, the famous medieval writer, found that her finances as a widow were disastrously tangled with various heirs who tried to claim her husband's property. In more peaceful times, the comfortably well-off widow was often seen as a relatively fortunate woman, able to reap the financial benefits of marriage without a man to lord over her. The poor widow, without property, was dependent on whatever charity she might find. Custom, law and the Church provided some protection for women's rights in the medieval period and, in particular, tried to make it acceptable for women to write their own wills.[12] But a powerful noble might rig juries or use force to make these laws meaningless. The prevailing view of historians is that women did have some property rights in medieval times. Research is still tentative on how widespread were the rights.

CHART

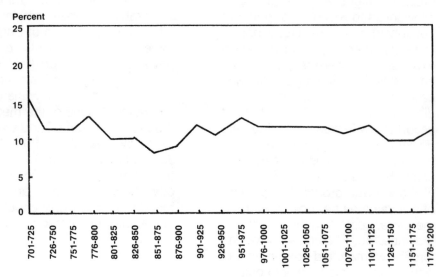

Percent of the total amount of property owned by women

___

[12]David Herlihy, "Land, Family and Women in Continental Europe, 701-1200," *Traditio*, Vol. 18 (New York: Fordham University Press, 1962), p. 109.

Points to Consider

1. What rights did *femmes soles* have to property?

   What rights did *femmes couvertes* have to property?

2. Generally what were the dower rights of widows?

   What ways could be taken to get around these dower rights?

3. How could a married woman occasionally become very wealthy?

4. Most of these limited property rights for women continued through the 19th century into European and American law. How would they compare to women's legal rights today?

5. What does this chart suggest about the amount of property owned outright by women in the era 701-1200 A.D. on the European continent?

   Does this evidence show that women owned considerable property? Were they equal to men in the amount they owned? From the readings, how might women have *controlled* property without actually owning it?

   What women probably *owned* land?

B. Women's Property Rights
Four Anglo-Saxon Wills

There is much that we will probably never know about women's property rights in European history. While various records do remain, historians cannot be sure that these represent what actually took place or whether written laws affected all classes equally. Wills indicate the operation of these property laws. Some wills still exist suggesting something of Anglo-Saxon women's property rights in England during that era. The following are excerpts from a few 10th and 11th century wills written by Anglo-Saxon women. Look over the excerpts and answer questions based on the evidence in the wills.

1. Could women control their own property? Could they dispose of it by last will and testament?

2. Did daughters inherit property or did it go to sons?

3. Did women seem to act as lords or were they in charge in any way?

4. What things seemed to be of particular value that were passed along in these wills? Of these possessions, which might still be included in wills today? Which things would no longer be passed along in wills?

5. What attitude toward religion is seen in the wills?

★ ★ ★ ★ ★ ★
The Will of Wulfgyth

"Here in this document it is made known how Wulfgyth grants after her death the things which Almighty God has allowed her to enjoy in life.

"First to my lord. . .And I grant the estate at Stisted, with the witness of God and my friends, to Christchurch for the sustenance of the monks in the community, on condition that my sons Aelfketel and Ketel may have the use of the estate for their lifetime; and afterwards the estate is to go to

Christchurch...for my soul and for my lord Aelfwine's and for the souls of all my children: and after their lifetime half the men[1] are to be free...

"And I grant to my sons Ulfketel and Ketel the estates at Walsingham and at Carleton and at Harling; and I grant to my two daughters, Gode and Bote, Saxlingham and Somerleyton. And to the church at Somerleyton sixteen acres of land and one acre of meadow. And to my daughter Ealdgyth I grant the estates at Chadacre and at Ashford, and the wood which I attached to the latter.....

"And I grant to Christ's altar at Christchurch a little gold crucifix, and a seat-cover. And I grant to St. Edmund's two ornamented horns. And I grant to St. Etheldreda's a woolen gown.[2]

★ ★ ★ ★ ★ ★

The Will of Aelfgifu

"This is Aelfgifu's request of her royal lord; she prays him for the love of God and for the sake of his royal dignity, that she may be entitled to make her will.

"Then she makes known to you, Sire, by your consent what she wishes to give to God's church for you and for your soul. First, she grants...the estate at Risborough just as it stands, except that, with your consent, she wishes that at each village every penally enslaved man who was subject to her shall be freed; and [she grants] two hundred mancuses[3] of gold to that minster and her shrine with her relics....

"And I grant to my royal lord the estates at Wing, Linslade, Haversham, Hatfield, Masworth and Gussage; and two armlets, each of a hundred and twenty mancuses, and a drinking-cup and six horses and as many shields and spears. And to the Aetheling the estate at Newnham and an armlet of thirty mancuses. And to the queen a necklace of a hundred and twenty mancuses and an armlet of thirty mancuses, and a drinking-cup.

"And I grant to Bishop Aethelwold the estate at Taeafersceat and pray him that he will always intercede for my mother and for me....

"And to my sister Aelfwaru I grant all that I have lent her; and to my brother's wife Aethelflaed the headband which I have lent her."[4]

★ ★ ★ ★ ★ ★

The Will of Wynflaed

"Wynflaed declares how she wishes to dispose of what she possesses, after her death. She bequeathes to the church her offering—...and the better of her offering-cloths, and her cross; and to the refectory two silver cups for the community; and as a gift for the good of her soul a mancus of gold to every servant of God....

"And she bequeathes to her daughter Aethelflaed her engraved bracelet and her brooch, and the estate at Ebbesborne and the title-deed as a perpetual inheritance to dispose of as she pleases; and she grants to her the men and the stock and all that is on the estate except what shall be given from it both in men and stock for the sake of her soul..."

---

[1] The men referred to were probably bonded or indentured servants to be allowed full freedom at that time.

[2] Excerpts from Dorothy Whitelock, ed. & tr., *Anglo-Saxon Wills* (Cambridge: Cambridge University Press, 1930), p. 85.

[3] Mancuses: An Anglo-Saxon measurement of gold or silver equal to 30 pence (or pennies).

[4] Whitelock, *Anglo-Saxon Wills*, p. 21.

This long will of over 1400 words lists very specific instructions as to whom would inherit which of her estates. She then says that:

"And Wulfwaru is to be freed, and she is to serve whom she pleases, And Wulfflaed is to be freed on condition that she serve Aethelflaed and Eadgifu. And she bequeathes to Eadgifu a woman-weaver and a seamstress the one called Eadgifu. the other called Aethelgifu. And Gerburg is to be freed and Miscin and Hi . . .and the daughter of Burhulf at Chinnock.
[here Wynflaed continues with a list of a number of bonded servants to be freed, ending with:]
"And if there be any penally enslaved man besides these whom she has enslaved, she trusts to her children that they will release him for her soul's sake."

She described in some detail how she wanted other estates, animal stock—such as "six oxen" and "four cows"—and bonded servants to be distributed to various relatives including a granddaughter, Eadgifu. Her will also included many specific bequests to individuals, such as:

two buffalo horns

a horse

a red tent

various ornamented and silver cups

gold

a set of bed clothing

her double badger-skin gown

linen cloth

a long hall tapestry

old filagree broach

gown and cap and headband

two large chests and clothes chest

a little spinning box

Although the end of the will seems to be missing, Wynflaed appears to be giving these final instructions in this last paragraph:

"Then she makes a gift to Aethelflaed of everything which is unbequeathed, books and such small things, and she trusts that she will be mindful of her soul. And there are also tapestries, one which is suitable for her, and the smallest she can give to her women. And she bequeathes to Cynelufu her share of the untamed horses which are with Eadmaer's. And to Aethelflaed she grants her. . .and the utensils and all the useful things that are inside, and also the homestead if the king grant it to her as King Edward granted it to Brihtwyn her mother. And Eadwold and his sister are to have her tame horses in common . . ."[5]

★ ★ ★ ★ ★ ★

The Will of Siflaed

"Here it is made known how Siflaed grants her possessions after her death. First to St. Edmund's for her dear soul, Marlingford, all except twenty acres and two wagonloads of wood and the woods over to the north. And my church is to be free and Wulfmaer my priest is to sing at it, he and his issue, so long as they are in holy orders. And free meadow to the church. And my men are to be free. And my St. Edmund be guardian there over the free property.

"He who wishes to alter this will, may he be excommunicated from Almighty God and from all his saints and from St. Edmund."[6]

---

[5]Whitelock, *Anglo-Saxon Wills*, p. 11-15.
[6]*Ibid.*, p. 93.

C. Women's Work
A Variety of Skills and Labors

It is striking looking back at history and seeing how much machinery has changed people's lives. Where there now are huge textile mills, there were, in medieval days, women working at spinning wheels. Where bakeries now begin in early morning to mass produce baked goods, the medieval housewife baked bread in shared village ovens. Where international hotels now encompass city blocks, the medieval lady or abbess took in travelers including the king's or queen's entourage. Where 30 ton combines now reap wheat fields, peasant men and women cut and gleaned and separated the wheat from the chaff with hand tools. Where cutting and sewing machines now mass produce clothes in a race to keep up with new styles, Chretien de Troyes, the 15th century poet, described in his poem, "Yvains" 300 sewing women, pale, bending their backs over their needles in despair.[1]

Thinking of the sheer physical activity and mental creativity that went into survival brings an added respect for the women and men of medieval times. Through an anonymous 14th century poet's eyes, we have a picture of the difficulty life might bring. Here are excerpts from the poem:

---

[1]Blanche Hinman Dow, *The Varying Attitude Toward Women in French Literature of the Fifteenth Century: The Opening Years* (New York: Publications of the Institute of French Studies, 1936), p. 62-63.

I saw a simple man me by.upon the plow bending,
His hood was full of holes.and his hair poked out,
His toes peeped in and out.as he the land trod,
His hose overhung his hocks.on every side,
All smothered in dirt.as he the plow followed;

This poor man besmired himself in dirt.almost to the ankle,
Four heifers went before him.that had become feeble,
Men could count all their ribs.so rueful [or sad] they were.
His wife walked him with.with a long goad,
In a short-cut coat.cut very high,
Wrapped in a winnowing sheet.to ward her from the weather,
Barefoot on the bare ice.so that the blood flowed.
And at the land's end lay.a little wooden bowl,
And therein lay a little child.
And twins of two years old.upon another side,
And all they sung a song.that was sorrowful to hear,
They cried all one cry.[2]

That women had considerable household responsibilities, such as cooking, making clothing, nursing the sick and feeding the family has been generally understood. Less generally recognized was that women filled a good many occupations outside of their homes. In the English language the suffix "ess" or "ster" was placed at the end of words to describe an occupation held by a woman.[3] Many of these words went out of use in the English language when these professions were closed to women in the 18th and 19th centuries. But the use of these words in medieval times demonstrated that they were occupations held by women.

Webster: woman weaver

Brewster, malster: woman beer maker

Baxter: woman baker

Lister, lyster: a woman who dyed cloth

Kempster: comber of wool

Laundress: woman washer of clothes

Seamstress: woman sewer

Governess: woman teacher

Spinster: woman spinner of cloth

The women who pursued these occupations sometimes did so in partnership with their husbands, but they often ran their own businesses. As suggested by this list of female occupations, England may have been unusual by having so many women in active trade. At least one Italian visitor expressed surprise at seeing so many women openly engaged in London trades.[4]

---

[2]Quoted in F. W. Tickner, *Women in English Economic History* (London: J.M. Dent, 1923), p. 19-20.

[3]Tickner, p. 53.

[4]Lacey Baldwin Smith, *A Tudor Tragedy: The Life and Times of Catherine Howard* (London: Jonathan Cape, 1961), p. 60.

But this Italian traveler may not have understood what was going on more quietly with Italian women. For example, women of Venice had a long history of economic enterprise. They:

- made loans to businesses
- invested in manufacturing
- put money into sea-going voyages[5]
- subsidized printing presses
- ran the lace industry[6]

Other Italian city-states had enterprising women. In Genoa, Florence, Milan and other areas, women were involved in the manufacturing of gold thread. The Genoese noblewomen took the lead, they invested money for gold thread and distributed it as far away as Syria in the Middle East. Apprentice systems were set up for women workers while more experienced women were hired by the noblewomen to run the shops. In Florence alone, there were over thirty of these workshops.[7]

The manufacture of cloth—whether gold, lace or plain—was often done by women. Men were also weavers, particularly of the heavier worsted cloth, but women took over nearly all the silk-weaving trade. As early as 13th century France, and later in England, women were apprenticed to each other in the silk trade.[8] A look at some 13th century French rules for these spinsters may give an idea of the rules that governed their occupation:

"Whosoever wishes to spin silk on the small spindle at Paris may do so freely, provided she works according to the uses and customs of the craft, which are as follows:

No one may or must work at this craft on any day appointed for a festival by the town community.

Women silk workers—collecting co-coons and weaving.

No one may or must take or have more than two apprentices only, nor take them for less than seven years of service.

No man or woman in the craft may or must hire another's apprentice or craftswoman until such time as she shall have done and completed her time.

No man or woman of the craft may or must take apprentices unless the agreement is made and recorded before [the courts].

---

[5]Stanley Chojnacki, "Patrician Women in Renaissance Venice," *Studies in the Renaissance,* Vol. XXI, p. 198.

[6]Edgcumbe Staley, *The Dogaressas of Venice* (London: T. Werner, Laurie, n.d.) p. 84-86, 290.

[7]William Bonds, "Genoese Noble Women and Gold Thread Manufacturing," *Medievalia and Humanistica,* 17 (1966), p. 79-81.

[8]Marian K. Dale, "The London Silkwomen of the Fifteenth Century," *Economic History Review,* 4 (October, 1933), p. 324-335.

If any craftswoman transfers her apprentice by sale, she cannot and must not take another apprentice until the full time has elapsed for which she took the apprentice whom she has sold.

When any apprentices have completed their time, or have bought themselves out, they must pay sixpence to [the courts], and swear on the saints or pledge their word to keep and practice the craft well and loyally...

If a woman from outside Paris comes to Paris to work at this craft, she may not and must not begin to work until such time as it is determined that she knows the craft...

The silk-spinsters are exempt from taxation when buying and selling things belonging to their craft."[9]

The course of work for women in these trades did not always go smoothly. For example, there were petitions by them to the king or queen to prevent foreign competition. Women apprentices often complained about their living conditions. Protests were made to convents that their cloth production created unfair competition to working women outside the convents.[10] Some customers did not pay on time—if ever. In other words, women had to have not only the skill to produce goods but also the knowledge to keep a business going.

In part, they were aided in solving their business problems by being guild members. Women were allowed to join some guilds— somewhat like today's trade unions...

• if the guild was designated for women.

• if they had been apprenticed as *a femme sole*.

Peasant women and men harvesting wheat

• if their husbands or fathers had been guild members.

Women who had a trade or shared a plot of land had some economic security. But there were women, single or widowed, who lived poorly as domestic workers or field hands. Domestic workers often got only board and room and no pay.[11] Women harvest workers were sometimes paid the same wages as men because they did the same work[12] but even this equal pay during the short harvest time did not last throughout the rest of the year.

[9]E. Dixon, "Craftswomen in the Livre des Metiers," *Economic Journal,* Vol. 5, (1895), p. 209-228.

[10]Ernest McDonnell, *The Beguines and Beghards in Medieval Culture* (New Brunswick: Rutgers University Press, 1954), p. 272.

[11]Alan Macfarlane, *The Origins of English Individualism* (New York: Cambridge University Press, 1978), p. 133.

[12]Annie Abram, "Women Traders in Medieval London," *Economic Journal,* Vol. 26 (1916), p. 280.

Women working at farm labor

Women in the medieval and Renaissance periods supported themselves and their families in various ways. Some, like Elizabeth Kirkey who sent $16,000 of merchandise out in one year, did very well. Others like those at the village of Montaillou, France, worked hard. These women lived by combing hemp and keeping house. They managed to survive but aged quickly.[13]

Points to Consider

1. What crafts were usually done by women?

2. What was the range of financial pay women received?

3. What were some of the rules of the French spinster guilds?

   Why do you think they had such rules?

4. Without machines, household tasks in medieval/Renaissance periods were time consuming, difficult work. Despite their heavy duties in home industries, what seems to have been some reasons that women worked outside their homes?

This Renaissance painting shows a wife and husband working as bankers.

[13]Emmanuel LeRoy Ladurie, *Montaillou: The Promised Land of Error* (New York: George Brazillier, 1978), p. 5.

D. Women as Healers
Doctors, Nurses and Midwives

In many cultures, much of the work of treating wounds, curing sickness and assisting at births has been women's work. Women have usually been in charge of child raising in families and, as such, were responsible for treating their children's wounds and illnesses. Family cooking and gardening have often been tasks of women. In these roles, women might learn the medicinal or curative properties of herbs as well as their use in food preparation. In medieval times, people were interested in the skills of warfare, as demonstrated in battles and tournaments. Women generally acted in defensive military roles—protectors of the castle-manor during wartime or as spectators at tournaments. It was most likely, then, that they were in charge of binding wounds of men and setting broken bones. Finally, women, as bearers of children, acted as sympathetic supporters for other women in childbirth. Some women came to be professional midwives making their living assisting at births.

Most women who practiced the art of healing were self-taught. Sometimes medical knowledge was passed down in a family—a father or mother trained their daughter in midwifery, in the art of surgery, or in knowledge of the medicinal properties of herbs. For example, Stephanie of Lyons, France, is recorded as a "medical" in a list that includes her father, a physician of the 13th century. A daughter of a German master surgeon in the 14th century was twice rewarded for healing soldiers' wounds. Many women learned the practice of midwifery by assisting their midwife-mothers.[1] On the other hand, many

---

[1]Muriel Joy Hughes, *Women Healers in Medieval Life and Literature* (New York: King's Crown Press, 1943), p. 88.

women learned their healing techniques by necessity, having to care for sick children, husbands or servants in isolated castles or manors. Some women were gifted with a talent for treating the sick and gained a special reputation for their ability to heal. They were asked to assist others during family illnesses or accidents. Often, these women practiced medicine as charity. Nuns or ladies of the manor might volunteer their services as healers. Some were paid, as was Cecilia of Oxford, hired as court surgeon to Queen Phillippa, wife of Edward III. Many villages had so-called wise women, paid to assist at births and to make herbal potions as medicines.[2]

Some women did read medical books that described theories on causes and cures of disease. Even though many women healers were not able to read medical books, through discussion with other healers, they probably gained knowledge of various widely accepted medical theories. Many of these theories dated back to antiquity. The Greek physician, Hippocrates (5th century B.C.) wrote that people's bodies were made up of four elements or "humors" (blood, phlegm, yellow bile and black bile) and these in balance supposedly determined the health of the body. The early medical writer and theorist, Galen, added to this theory of humors, the notion that people's bodies were also regulated by "complexions."[3] Most medieval physicians believed in astrology— that the positions of the moon, stars and other heavenly bodies had a serious influence on health.[4] Mixed in with their fantastic superstitious medical theories, writers such as Hippocrates and Galen, made some serious contributions to the science of medicine. Although medieval people might have some knowledge of these theories, probably more useful in curing the sick were the practical, folk medicine remedies and methods developed by trial and error.[5] Most women healers practiced folk medicine. These healers were called empirics (those who learned from experience and from other practitioners).

Until the growth of universities in the 13th century, women medical practitioners were treated fairly equally with men. There were almost no restrictions on who practiced medicine and the reputation of a particular healer depended on her/his practical ability to cure the sick.[6] But in the 12th century, universities were organized in Italy and spread into other parts of Europe. The practice of medicine was slowly turned over to university trained people. Reputations of the empirics (those people trained by experience) declined. The development of university trained physicians had serious implications for women healers:

- Women were almost all empirics because only a few women were allowed admission to universities.

- Regulations were passed that required physicians and surgeons to be licensed guild members. Women were usually discouraged from joining guilds.

---

[2]Jean Donnison, *Midwives and Medical Men* (New York: Schocken Books, 1977), p. 2.

[3]Hughes, *Women Healers*, p. 20.

[4]*Ibid.*, p. 21.

[5]*Ibid.*, p. 21-22.

[6]*Ibid.*, p. 62.

Fewer women became doctors during the later Middle Ages. Even so, it may seem as if these new requirements for university training and licensing of doctors would improve medical practice. This did not necessarily prove to be true. Medical students at universities did receive more theoretical training. They were required to read the famous medical works of history such as those of Hippocrates and Galen. However, as was seen earlier, much of this time-honored theory they studied was silly and not at all scientific. On the other hand, the folk medicine of the empirics was often based on observation and practice—cures that worked were repeated. Much folk medicine was also based on superstition; some empirics were simply charlatans or frauds who took advantage of ill or desperate people. Still, the best practical folkhealers probably were at least as good as university trained doctors of the Middle Ages. As empirics, most women were forced out of medicine as the academic doctors took over. These university trained doctors often had little practical experience. They frequently used long Latin terms to impress their patients, but also to cover up their own ignorance. Thus, by insisting on university training for doctors while barring women empirics from training, valuable folk medicine and experience was lost in the interests of so-called science. A better path might have been to combine the practical medicine of the experienced empirics with theoretical, academic medicine.

Women healers did continue to practice medicine, often without official approval. Probably each village of medieval Europe had wise women known to have knowledge of herbs, cures and ointments. Often their skills included use of folk magic—incantations, amulets and charms—the line between superstitious use of medicine and magic was sometimes a fine one.

A few universities in Italy did admit some women students and several outstanding women practiced as academically trained physicians. For example, Costanza Colend of Naples and Maestra Antonia of Florence were recorded as medical lecturers and university trained doctors.[7] Women in most societies have assisted at the births of babies. Older experienced women were called upon so frequently that those with special abilities became paid professional midwives. The most famous group of medieval midwives were those from Salerno, Italy, in the 11th century. Though some of them may have attended lectures at the medical school or been from families of physicians, they seem to have been empirics who formed a strong organization.[8] The most famous of them, Trotula, marks the transition from ancient to modern medicine.[9] She wrote two medical books in which she described simple, practical procedures praised by modern doctors.[10]

In one essay Trotula told why she became interested in gynecology and midwifery. While she accepted some ancient assumptions about the physical weakness of women, she recognized that women might be more comfortable being treated by women doctors:

---

[7]Hughes, p. 63.

[8]*Ibid.*, p. 100.

[9]See: H.P. Bayon, "Trotula and the Ladies of Salerno: A contribution to the Knowledge of the Transition Between Ancient and Medieval Physick," *Proceedings of the Royal Society of Medicine,* Vol. 33 (June, 1940), p. 471-475.

[10]Hughes, *Women Healers,* p. 106.

"Since women are by nature weaker than men, it is reasonable that sicknesses more often abound in them expecially around the organs involved in the work of nature. Since these organs happen to be in a retired location, women on account of their modesty and the fragility and delicacy of the state of these parts dare not reveal the difficulties of their sicknesses to a male doctor. Wherefore I, pitying their misfortunes and at the instigation of a certain matron, began to study carefully the sicknesses which most frequently trouble the female sex."[11]

Most midwives did not have Trotula's high reputation. Many were simply experienced, village women who helped at births for a fee. Many may have used doubtful methods. Some were physically filthy and mentally ignorant. Others gained legitimate respect for their skills. However, as 13th century surgeon's guilds developed, to which few women were allowed membership, men took over as surgeons. Guild surgeons controlled the use of all surgical instruments, such as forceps, used to assist at difficult births. Under these regulations, midwives had to call in surgeons in difficult cases. This had negative results because new man-midwives knew little about normal childbirth as they were called in only for the very worst cases. Therefore, experienced women were restricted in their practice of midwifery.[12]

Under one circumstance the midwife was allowed to use surgical instruments—and that a tragic one. If the mother died during delivery, the midwife performed a Caesarean section to extract the baby from the womb. This was a commandment of the Roman Catholic Church so that the baby would not die unbaptized.

A 15th century rhymed instruction to parish priests tells them to have a midwife assist:

*"And if the woman then die
Take the midwife that show he
For to undo her with a knife
And for to save the child's life
And he that is christened be,
For that is a deed of charity."*[13]

The midwife was not only directed to save the child by extreme measures, but if no priest were available she was also authorized to baptize the baby. Because of religious, as well as medical duties, various provisions were made to insure that she was of "good character." By the 17th century, English midwives were required to take an oath and have witnesses to their moral character. The oath was made up of 15 separate provisions. A few selections from the oath indicate the sensitive nature of the medieval/Renaissance midwife's calling:

Midwife's Oath

"You shall swear, first, that you shall be diligent and faithful and ready to help every women laboring with child as well the poor as the rich; and that in time or necessity you shall not forsake the poor women to go to the rich.

"You shall neither cause nor suffer any woman to name or put any father to the child, but only him which is the very true father thereof indeed.

"You shall not in any wise use or exercise any manner of witchcraft, charm or sorcery, invocation or other prayers.

---

[11]Quoted in *Ibid.*, p. 105.

[12]Donnison, *Midwives,* p. 2.

[13]Quoted in Middle English in: *Ibid.*, p. 3.

A midwife assists at a birth while friends support a woman in labor.

"You shall not give any counsel or minister any herb, medicine, or potion, or any other thing, to any woman being with child whereby she should destroy or cast out that she goeth withal before her time.

"You shall not enforce any woman being with child by any pain or by any ungodly ways or means to give you any more for your pains or labor in bringing her to bed, than they would otherwise do.

"You shall not consent, agree, give, or keep counsel that any woman be delivered secretly . . . "[14]

As can be seen in these provisions, midwives might be called on to perform acts then considered theologically or socially questionable. In cases of adultery or unmarried pregnancy, the midwife might learn the father's name during the drama of delivery and be asked not to reveal it. She might be asked to end unwanted pregnancies. She might be tempted to use charms or witchcraft practices in difficult cases. Some midwives were accused of taking dead fetuses for use in magical potions.

As university trained man-midwives slowly gained acceptance, women midwives tended to lose ground. During the witchcraft crazes and hunts of the 14th-17th centuries, midwives were often accused of sorcery. Whether or not these accusations were false, a feeling remained that women-midwives were ignorant or dangerous. A few women-midwives were educated and wrote books on midwifery. In the 17th century Louise Bourgeois, midwife to the Queen of France, midwife Justina Siegemundin of the Russian Court and Jane Sharp of London wrote valuable works on the topic. However, in general, after the late 17th century, man-midwives

gained at the expense of women. Still, for modesty's sake, women patients often preferred women-midwives and man-midwives were sometimes required to assist the women blind. One can imagine how inadequate this medical technique was as a method of assisting at deliveries. Even so, university trained men came to dominate the field of midwifery, especially in England, and helped to discredit women midwives. Notions that women midwives were ignorant and often drunken persisted even though there continued to be many midwives of good character. In the late 18th century an English woman, Margaret Stephens, a respected midwife, defended her female colleagues against these charges:

"Those who have found it in their interest to bring midwives into disrepute have charged them with intemperance, and even obscenity. How being a midwife should make women possess such vices, is to me a mystery. I know no way of life in which a woman can be engaged, that is more calculated to fix sentiments of piety and morality upon the mind, nor have I ever been acquainted with any midwife who did not possess them."[15]

Elizabeth Nihell, another 18th century midwife, summarized the plight of women healers and said that no matter how thoughtful, skilled and reputable of character a woman midwife was, people felt they could pay her little *"for no other reason on earth, but because she is not a man."*[16]

---

[14]James Hobson Aveling, *English Midwives, Their History and Prospects* (London: Hugh K. Elliott, 1967, 1872), p. 90-92.

[15]Donnison, *Midwives,* p. 34.

[16]Quoted in *Ibid.,* p. 35.

94

Points to Consider

1. In what ways might academic medicine have been no better than folk or empiric medicine? In what ways was it perhaps worse, at least in medieval times?

2. Who were a few of the famous women medical practitioners of medieval times?

   Where did they receive their training?

   For what reasons do you think their names have come down to us as part of historical record?

3. What do you think of Trotula's reasons for wanting to be a midwife?

   What things in her statement do you agree or sympathize with?

   What not?

4. If you were a late medieval/Renaissance woman why might you prefer being attended by a woman midwife when you gave birth rather than a man-midwife?

   Thinking back to the role of the guild surgeon, man-midwife, why do you think man-midwives were often greeted by women in childbirth by expressions of horror and fear?

5. What religious functions did midwives sometimes perform?

   Why?

6. In the Midwife's Oath what specific things were midwives instructed to swear not to do in the course of their practice?

   Why do you think that midwives might be required to have such a long oath?

7. What specifically may have led to a decline of women midwives by the 18th century?

8. In the last chapter of this book the witch hunts of medieval/Renaissance Europe are discussed.

   What do you think might be some of the reasons that midwives were singled out as one group frequently accused of being witches?

Chapter 4
The Social Setting
of Women in
Medieval/Renaissance
Europe

A. Family Characteristics Affecting Women

Recent scholarship—using computers to study population statistics in historical records—has developed some new views of the medieval European family. Historians had thought that the typical medieval European family, whether noble or peasant:

- married off children early.
- was composed of married or widowed adults and children, as virtually all people married eventually.
- had developed the usual ties of affection between parents and children.
- had three or more generations living together in an extended family.

New scholarship, however, has turned up evidence that questions these conclusions and there are lively controversies over these new theories among historians. The following sections describe the implications of these new theories and how they change historians' ideas of how medieval/Renaissance women lived.

NORTHERN EUROPEANS MARRIED LATE

The nobility probably married their eldest sons and daughters early, but unlike what was earlier thought, the rest of the population seems to have married rather late—between the ages of 25-30. This late marriage age made Northern Europe unique when compared to other cultures of the world.[1] Why the delayed marriage age? Historians are not

---

[1]Lawrence Stone, *The Family, Sex and Marriage in England 1500-1800* (New York: Harper & Row, 1977), p. 50.

sure, but one historian has suggested that it was a situation caused by economic considerations— "no land, no marriage."[2] Unlike other societies in which the family unit owned property, Northern European families seemed to have expected most of their children to go out and support themselves. Family property might be willed to various children but primogeniture meant that it usually went to the eldest son. Historians speculate that this late marriage age may have allowed women more opportunities to acquire an education. They also might have had better health because childbearing would have been delayed and fewer children born.

SOME EUROPEANS NEVER MARRIED

Formerly, the belief held was that, except for nuns and monks, almost all medieval people married. More recent demographic (population) studies have shown that, in some countries at least 10-12 percent of the population *never* married[3] and other people did not go through formal church marriages. The Roman Catholic Church carried on a long struggle to have monogamous marriage be the accepted practice. In various groups before Christianity, such as the Franks and the Celts, polygyny (a husband with more than one wife) was a custom. Even the famous Christian emperor, Charlemagne, had several wives or concubines and many children. Early medieval Merovingian and Carolingian royal history is full of stories of wives set aside—sent to convents or even murdered—so husbands could take new wives. On the social level of the lesser nobility and among peasants, marriages were informally arranged, partners

taking vows without a priest. Sometimes witnesses assured that the marriage took place. At other times a man or woman claimed that a marriage had taken place but there was no witness to prove that vows had been made. The Church tried to strengthen the rules of what was a proper marriage ceremony to protect the interests of pregnant women who claimed to be married. For example, in England in 1076, the Winchester Council set down the following guidelines:

- There should be no sexual intercourse before betrothal (a formal promise of marriage).

- There should be an announcement of banns (a public declaration) a few weeks before the final wedding ceremony.

- The exchange of vows should be performed by a priest.[4]

But medieval times were often chaotic and priests not always available, so the custom of private exchange of vows continued. Controversies about who was legally married continued to embroil law courts. Pregnant women were especially vulnerable in cases of dispute over the validity of their marriages. If it were decided that they had not been married, they might be socially ostracized and left without financial support.

---

[2]Alan Macfarlane, *The Origins of English Individualism: The Family, Property and Social Transition* (New York: Cambridge University Press, 1978), p. 156.

[3]*Ibid.*, p. 160.

[4]Michael Sheehan, "Marriage Theory and Practice in the Conciliar Legislation and Diocesan Statutes of Medieval England," *Medieval Studies*, Vol. 45, 1978, p. 408-460.

EUROPEAN CHILDREN WERE NOT CONSIDERED SPECIAL

In the later Victorian period of 19th century Europe, homes abounded with pictures of sweet children, and motherhood was seen as the special blessing of womanhood. Paintings from the Renaissance also conveyed this image. For example, in this painting of Mary by Raphael, the Madonna smiles gently at her child. Recent historians present a darker picture of medieval/Renaissance childhood. The controversial French historian, Philip Aries, pointed out in his book, *Centuries of Childhood,* that childhood itself may have been a fairly recent invention. The medieval French language, for example, had words for baby but none for child or teenager.[5] Medieval paintings show children as little adults, pictured as defective creatures until they grew up. Perhaps the high mortality rate for children had something to do with the view that children were either babies or on their way to adulthood. One study of infant mortality indicates that one third of the infants who survived birth died within fourteen days.[6]

There may have been reasons other than the hardship of birth and disease for the high infant mortality rate during the medieval period. Infanticide seems to have been practiced as a part of population control, as it had been earlier in Greek and Roman history. Generally, infanticide was carried out by neglecting the infant's needs rather than by actively killing the child, as this was seen as murder. For example, the people who lived on the West Frisian Islands believed that if a child was once fed, it must be saved. If not fed, however, the baby could be left to die. One medieval Frisian woman, Liafburga, who became a saint of the Church, was saved only when a servant put food into her mouth.[7] Once fed, it was considered necessary to keep her alive. When population control was practiced through infanticide, girl babies were more likely to die because boys were commonly considered more desirable. For example, in 15th century Florence, Italy, the ratios of males to females were as follows:

Age	Boys	Girls
0 to 1	114.60	100
1	118.43	100
2	119.28	100
3	119.50	100
4	119.42	100

In wealthy families the ratio at age four was even wider, with 124.56 boys to every 100 girls.[8] One of the reasons for more female deaths was that it was often customary to nurse male babies twice as long as female babies, thus giving boys a better nutritional start.[9]

Why was infanticide, in particular, female infanticide, practiced? Economic pressure seemed to be the primary motive—too many mouths for too little land. Social customs also played a part; for example, the high male to female ratio in the statistics of the upper

---

[5]Philip Aries, *Centuries of Childhood.* (New York: Vintage Books, 1960), p. 28-33.

[6]Stone, p. 68.

[7]Emily Coleman, "Infanticide in the Early Middle Ages," in *Women in Medieval Society,* Susan Mosher Stuard, ed., (Philadelphia: University of Pennsylvania Press, 1976), p. 58.

[8]Richard Trexler, "Infanticide in Florence," *History of Childhood Quarterly,* Vol. 25 (May, 1973), p. 101.

[9]Coleman, p. 60.

classes of Florence may reflect the large increase in the size of dowries during these years. A costly dowry system that took money away from the family may have been one reason for female infanticide.

EUROPEAN CHILDREN AWAY FROM HOME

Unlike earlier ideas that European families were close, European customs actually seemed to encourage distance between the parents and the child. For example, while peasant mothers nursed their children, women of even moderate circumstances generally did not. Instead, children were given to "wet nurses,"[10] nearby or in the countryside. Why this custom became commonplace is somewhat unclear. Wet-nursing was present in the medieval period and well established by the 18th century. For example, in 1780 a report said that of the 21,000 Parisian children born annually, 1,000 were breast-fed by their mothers, 1,000 had wet nurses nearby and the rest, 19,000, were raised in the countryside. [11] There seems to have been a curious conflicting cultural attitude toward the custom of wet-nursing. While paintings and sculptures of fat, sweet babies are found, in truth, babies were usually sent away from their homes to be cared for by wet nurses. A woman like Margaret of Navarre was known throughout Europe for her tolerance and kindness, yet her daughter was raised away from her and few affectionate traces between them may be seen in their letters to each other. And the wet nurses? We know little of their views of their charges or even what happened to their own children while raising other children.

In some countries, such as England, children between the ages of 7 and 14 were sent away to live. Some of these children were apprenticed to various guild members to learn a trade. Records of the 13th and 14th centuries show such actions. Agnes Tikhyll, daughter of William Tikhyll, saddler, apprenticed for 14 years to William Celler, citizen and wire-drawer, to learn the trade of cardmaker.[12] Agnes' age is not mentioned in this record, but girls were usually apprenticed at about 12 years, boys at 14.[13] It was not only the lower economic classes that sent their children to other families to learn. There was also a tradition of sending upper class sons and daughters to wealthier establishments to gain wider experiences. The courts, like that of Queen Claude of France, became places to send young girls to be educated. Often, young women became attendants to great ladies, to wait on them with the added opportunity of making a good marriage. At one time, Queen Claude had 300 girls under her supervision. The career of Bess Hardwick, who became one of the wealthiest women in British history, began when she was sent as a virtually penniless child into a well-established household. There she learned how to manage a household

---

[10]Women who had had a child and nursed a stranger's child for them.

[11]Elizabeth Badinter, "Love Plus, the History of Maternal Love," *Time*, July 28, 1980, p. 78.

[12]Dorothy Gardiner, *English Girlhood at School* (London: Oxford University Press, 1929), p. 287.

[13]Dr. Kathryn Reyerson, University of Minnesota, from her research at Montpellier, France.

and found the man who became the first of her four well-to-do husbands.[14] Anne Boleyn, mother of Elizabeth I, and her sister Mary came from better circumstances than Bess, but they were sent off to the French court to learn manners and to lead a more sophisticated life style.

Another custom which separated children from their parents was the system of wardships. According to feudal ideas, land belonged to the king or queen. Land was given to nobles who in turn provided military services and taxes, but the queen or king could take the land back if these services stopped. When the father of a family died before his children reached the age of majority (an age that might be from 14-25), the ruler had rights to the man's property before the heirs. This meant that a mother might not control the fate of her own children.

Often, children would become wards of the crown. Anyone with enough money might buy a wardship from the ruler and then he would control the child. This control might include determining his/her education and choice of a marriage partner. Until the age of majority, the ruler or owner of the wardship would also get the profits of the child's estate. Mothers would often try to buy the wardship of their children but did not usually have the means to do so. For example, in Tudor England, out of seventy wardships studied, only ten went to mothers.[15] Sometimes the child would be left with the mother for a period of nurture until age six or seven, or sometimes longer if the owner of the wardship had no better place to raise the ward.[16] This whole custom came to be criticized as unfair to women who first lost their husbands, then, in turn, lost their children. In Shakespeare's play,

"All's Well that Ends Well," a mother protests the taking away of her son as a ward . . . *"In delivering my son from me, I bury a second husband."*[17] Not all medieval women lived on feudal lands that could be taken back by rulers. Some women lived on socage (lands free of feudal duties) and did not have to face the threat of wardships. But the custom of wardships frequently separated mother and child.

FEW THREE GENERATION FAMILIES

Another recent finding about medieval life is that the nuclear family of parent and child thought to be a modern development was actually present throughout most of European history. While some large households also included grandparents and certainly servants, tenants and others living within them, generally the family seems to have been a nuclear one.[18] Research of a sample of English households from 1574-1821, for example, showed that less than six percent were made up of more than two generations.[19] This may have meant that older widowed or single women were not supported within a joint family.

---

[14]David Durant, *Bess of Hardwick: Portrait of an Elizabethan Dynast* (London: Weidenfeld and Nicolson, 1977), p. 9.

[15]Joel Hurstfield, *The Queens Wards: Wardship and Marriage Under Elizabeth I* (Cambridge: Harvard University Press, 1958), p. 125.

[16]Sue Sheridan Walker, "Widow and Ward: The Feudal Law of Child Custody in Medieval England," *Feminist Studies*, Vol. 3, No. 3/4, (1976), p. 106.

[17]Quoted in Hurstfield, p. 129.

[18] Stone, p. 23-24.

[19]Macfarlane, p. 138.

Medieval family gathers together for supper.

★ ★ ★ ★ ★ ★

What, then are the conclusions of these more recent family history theories? There are not many clear answers yet. Letters often show strong ties of affection between parents and children. For example, the loyalty between Catherine of Aragon and her daughter Mary was maintained throughout both trying and dangerous times as their correspondence demonstrates. There are poems that showed real affection, like those of Vittoria Colona to her husband, illustrating love between wife and husband.[20] But there are also signs of a commonly expected distance between family members. For example, Lady Jane Grey's description of her mother's physical abuse to her or the formal, rather cold letters exchanged between Margaret Paston and her daughter, Elizabeth, illustrate many different sorts of family arrangements in European history. There was the polygynous Charlemagne whose daughters were either too precious or too political to marry and so remained single and at home. There were families involved in criminal gangs—one third of all group crimes in England in the 14th century were committed by families.[21] There were single parent families like that of the widow Anne Bacon, who lectured to her son, Francis Bacon, and his wild friend Essex, to mend their ways, to quit party and theater going.[22] There were families like that of Thomas More, philosopher and advisor to Henry VIII of England, in which all members were respected and encouraged. Historians are just beginning to understand how complicated family history was in Europe and how these various family arrangements affected women's lives.

Points to Consider

1. What do the new views of European medieval family history suggest about the following:

    Mother/child relationships?

    Female infanticide?

    Three generation families?

2. How did the sentence from William Shakespeare's play *"All's Well that Ends Well"*—*"In delivering my son from me, I bury a second husband."*— relate to the practice of wardship?

3. What were some of the economic pressures which made either for late marriage or none at all in medieval times?

---

[20]Maud Jerrold, *Vittoria Colonna* (Freeport, New York: Books for Libraries Press, 1969), (1906), p. 12-13.

[21]Stone, p. 95.

[22]Pearl Hogrefe, *Women of Action in Tudor England* (Ames: Iowa State University Press, 1977), p. 48-49.

B. Jewish Women in a Christian World

Introduction

Throughout medieval times, the one consistent factor that gave unity to politically divided Europe was the Christian religion—in Western Europe represented by the Roman Catholic Church. Some Christian groups challenged the supremacy and authority of the Roman Church but these had little permanent success. There was one large minority group of Europeans who were not Christian believers. They were neither Catholics nor challengers to Catholicism. These were the Jews who had emigrated from Palestine in the Middle East at the time of the Roman conquests and become early European settlers.

In 69 A.D. the Roman Emperor Tiberius destroyed the Jewish temple in Jerusalem and dispersed the Jews of Palestine into exile. Many of these Jewish exiles made their way to Europe. Jews were not considered heretics[1] by the Roman Catholic Church as they had never been Christians. Therefore, while it was an objective of the Church to convert Jews and baptize them as Christians, they were not persecuted as heretics. They were accepted, at least to some extent, as sharing similar beliefs in the early books of the Bible with Christians. Beginning with Pope Gregory the Great in the 6th century, Roman Catholic Popes issued bulls (orders) instructing their Christian subjects not to abuse members of the Jewish minority. The need for these frequent bulls indicates that the Christian majority often took advantage of its power over this minority group. However,

---

[1]Heretics: In medieval times these were Christians whose beliefs were contrary to the doctrines of the Roman Catholic Church. Usually they joined together to create a sect of like believers outside standard Catholicism. Often they were vigorously persecuted by the Catholic church.

European Jews were fairly well protected from abuse until the time of the religious Crusades in the 11th and 12th centuries. As the Crusaders organized to march against the Muslims who controlled the Holy Land of Palestine, the idea seems to have taken hold that the non-Christians in Europe, the Jews, should also either be converted or destroyed.

From the time of the Crusades to modern times, European Jews have periodically been singled out for persecution. Various forms of this persecution differed, depending on time and place.

- After the Crusades, Jews came to live in specified areas of towns called ghettos,[2] often walled and crowded.

- Jews were usually not permitted to own land and, as land owners were expected to provide military services, they were kept out of government or military service.

- Jews were often singled out as scapegoats for blame in time of trouble or disaster. For example, during the terrible plague that began in 1348 called the Black Death, Jews were accused of causing the epidemic. Thousands were cruelly burned to death in the ghettos of Europe by angry Christian mobs.

While these factors affected both Jewish women and men, there were two questions that pertained specifically to Jewish women:

What were their expected roles within their own Jewish community?

How did the fact of this periodic persecution affect Jewish women's lives and roles?

Women's Roles Within the European Jewish Community

The survival of Judaism (the religion of the Jews) in exile had come to center around Biblical scholarship. Central to this learning was the study of Torah or the Law and the study of the Talmud, the sixty volumes of interpretations and commentaries on the law that were written in early medieval times. Scholarship was the most honored activity of European Jewish life. It was through study that teachers or Rabbis would gain the knowledge of Judaism to guard and preserve the religious observances of the exiled community.

Generally, Jewish women were excluded from this scholarship. Although fathers were directed to teach their sons Torah, no mention was made of teaching daughters. In fact, some commentators, such as Rabbi Eliezer in the 1st century, claimed that women should not be taught Torah. Rabbi Eliezer vehemently declared, *"If any man teach his daughter Torah it is as though he taught her lechery."*[3]

Even if Jewish women were not strictly forbidden from studying Torah it was unlikely that they would do so. No one was directed to teach girls and no one obliged them to study.

---

[2]The first required ghetto was in Italy in the 1500's but by then most Jews were living in ghettos, by force of custom and official encouragement.

[3]Quoted in Leonard Swidler, *Women in Judaism: The Status of Women in Formative Judaism* (Metuchen, NJ: The Scarecrow Press, 1976), p. 93.

One exceptional woman in early European Judaism did study Torah and her commentaries on the law are recorded in the Talmud. Her name was Beruria. She was the daughter of a Rabbi and wife of an important 2nd century Rabbi. Exactly who taught her is not known, but she seems to have been extremely wise and brilliant.

In accounts about Beruria she was described as always disputing and discussing the law with male students—she was also seen as superior in intellect to these men. Pictured as an exception to the women of her time who were not educated in Torah, at least one story shows that she resented the treatment of women as second class citizens. She lashed out sarcastically to remind a Rabbi that by law, men were instructed not to speak much with women as they were considered too *"lightheaded:"*

"...Rabbi Jose the Galilean was once on a journey when he met Beruria. 'By what road,' he asked her, 'do we go to Lydda?' 'Foolish Galilean,' she replied, 'did not the Sages say this: Engage not in much talk with women? You should have asked: By which to Lydda?..."[4]

If the Biblical scholar Beruria was an exception, what were the expected roles for Jewish women in medieval Europe? According to Jewish law, women had a different set of obligations from men. For example, they were exempt from many religious duties that fell to men. Women were not required to say prayers after meals, to be present at the sound of the Shofar (Ram's horn) on New Years, or to say the Shema (great Jewish prayer), "Hear, O Israel, the Lord our God, the Lord is One" twice a day. Exemptions from religious

Jewish mother serves seder meal at Passover as shown in this medieval drawing.

duties may have been allowed because of their heavy household chores or because during menstruation and after childbirth women were considered ritually impure. Eventually many of these exemptions became prohibitions. Women were, thus, excluded from certain important religious observances.[5]

Jewish women were also not counted toward a minyan—the ten Jewish men required as a minimum to conduct the daily services. This restriction may have come about because women came to be segregated to a women's court in later temples. They also come to be separated by a barrier or grill in synagogues—the Jewish meeting halls for worship and study. It seems

---

[4]*Ibid.*, p. 102.

[5]*Ibid.*, p. 83-84.

109

that women were not segregated before the building of the last "Temple of Herod" (begun in c. 19 B.C.)[6] in Jerusalem. By medieval times, women were segregated from men in synagogues and so could not contribute to the quorum required for communal prayer.

On the other hand, specific religious duties became obligations for Jewish women to perform.

- *Laws of niddah.* Women were to avoid any physical contact with their husbands during their menstrual periods. Before a husband and wife resumed sexual intercourse after her menstruation ended she was to immerse herself in the mikvah or communal bath.[7]

- *The taking of hallah or dough.* The first part of the daily bread dough was set aside and thrown into the fire by the woman of the household as a symbolic sacrifice in rememberance of the destruction of the temple at Jerusalem.

- *The kindling of the Sabbath lights.* This was a female obligation performed within the family. If a woman neglected this duty she was to light an extra candle every Friday for the rest of her life.[8]

All three of these religious obligations were accomplished outside the Temple or synagogue. None involved study or extensive prayer and only the lighting of the Sabbath candles seemed a central ritual duty.

Jewish Women's Roles Outside of Judaism

By medieval times, Jewish women had limited ritualistic roles within Judaism. In other aspects of medieval Jewish life, women slowly gained importance. These opportunities for Jewish women related both to the nature of Jewish life and to the fact of periodic persecution of Jews as a minority group.

As life in the ghettos of Europe became increasingly restricted and difficult, Jewish family life frequently gained social, religious and economic importance. For example, given severe religious persecution, both prayer and study were conducted within the home rather than at a public synagogue. The traditionally important roles for women were those of housewife and mother. According to Jewish law, men were commanded to marry. Unlike the Christian tradition of celibate nuns and monks, there was no honored place for unmarried women or men in Judaism. Couples were instructed to have children as a religious duty. Finally, a medieval Jewish family was often crucial economically because of frequently severe restrictions on occupations allowed Jews. Most medieval Jews were very poor and family survival depended on both mother and father working to provide a family income.

One occupation that Jewish women engaged in during medieval times was that of lending money. Since Christians were forbidden to charge interest on money loaned, this was one occupation in which Jews could profit. Many Jewish women were involved as lenders.

---

[6]*Ibid.*, p. 88-89.

[7]Many societies and various religions adhere to rules that segregate menstruating women. The ancient origin of these customs originally indicated the awe with which people held the reproductive abilities of women.

[8]For a discussion of these three female duties see: Rabbi Sally Priesand, *Judaism and The New Woman* (New York: Behrman House, 1975), p. 23-25.

One historian has shown that about half the loans made in an area of 13th century France were made by women.[9] Usually, these loans were rather small and were made to Christian women for their immediate needs. One such loan, for example, was made to a woman named Margha de Vermans, who needed to raise money to pay a fine to free her husband from jail.[10] It is clear from records in both England and France that it was commonplace for Jewish women to be occupied in lending money as a means to help support their families.[11]

There were Jewish women skilled in many different trades. For example, a letter survives written to the famous Italian, Caterina Sforzia, from a Jewish woman named Anna, a manufacturer of cosmetics. At the time of the letter, Caterina was 45, had borne eight children, buried three husbands, but still desired to maintain her *"fair and fine complexion."* To do so she sought Anna's advice and received this businesslike reply:

"To the most illustrious Madonna, Caterina de Reariis, Sfortia Vicecomitissa, Countess de Imola, my most honored Patroness. Wherever she may be.

"Permit me, most illustrious Madonna, to commend myself to you and to send you greetings. Messer Antonio Melozo, Esquire, has been here on behalf of your Highness to inquire of me if I will not give him as many kinds of facial cream as I have.

"To begin with, I gave him a black salve which removes roughness of the face, and makes the flesh supple and smooth. Put this salve on at night, and allow it to remain on till the morning. Then wash yourself with pure river water; next bathe your face in the lotion that is called Acqua da Canicare; then put on a dab of this white cream and then take less than a chickpea grain of this powder, dissolve it in the lotion called Acqua Dolce and put it on your face, the thinner the better.

"The black salve costs four carlini an ounce; the Acqua de Canciere, four carlini a small bottle. The salve, that is the white cream, costs eight carlini an ounce; the powder, one gold ducat an ounce, and the Acqua Dolce will cost you a gold ducat for a small bottle.

"Now if your illustrious Highness will apply these things, I am quite sure that you will order from us continually.

"I commend myself to your Highness always.

"Rome, the 15th of March, 1508.

> *Your Highness' servant*
> *Anna The Hebrew*

[P.S.]The black salve is bitter. If it should happen to go into the mouth, you may be assured that it is nothing dangerous; the bitterness comes from the aloes in it." [To poison one's enemies was not uncommon then!][12]

Some medieval/Renaissance Jewish women gained an education. One woman, Rebecca Tiktiner, became a learned translator of

---

[9]William Chester Jordan, "Jews on Top: Women and the Availability of Consumption Loans in Northern France in the Mid-Thirteenth Century" *Journal of Jewish Studies*, Vol. 29 (1978), p. 53.

[10]*Ibid.*, p. 46.

[11]See, M. Adler *Jews of Medieval England* (London: Oxford University Press, 1939).

[12]Jacob R. Marcus, *The Jew in the Medieval World, A Source Book 315-1791* (Cincinnati: The Sinai Press, 1938), p. 399-400.

Hebrew works into Judeo-German.[13] She also became a preacher and author of a book first published in Poland in 1609.[14] Some other women became scribes, such as the 13th century Italian Jewish woman, Paula Dei Mansi, who copied and translated Biblical commentaries. Another scribe was Frommet Arwyller, whose copy of a book is now in the rare book collection of the National Library of Paris.[15]

During the Italian Renaissance, Jewish women's involvement in literature and the arts became commonplace. Jews had been driven out of Spain by the Inquisition in the late 15th century. Many of them settled in Italy and took advantage of the high degree of learning and the arts of the Italian Renaissance. Some Jewish women became medical doctors, such as Perna of Fano; others became entertainers, such as Madonna Bellina who *"sang like a thousand nightingales."* Many were teachers, scholars, and a Jewish school for girls—a Talmud Torah—was operating in Rome by 1475.[16] Devora Ascarelli was one of the first Italian Jewish women poets, and Sara Coppia Sullam represents the classic Renaissance person—she wrote poetry, sang while performing on lute or harpsichord and read in five languages. She started a famous literary salon in Venice where she and her wealthy husband were the center of Venetian cultural life.[17]

These are just a few of the many distinguished medieval and Renaissance Jewish women. Most Jewish women, while not achieving the fame of these, worked in numerous occupations. Like many Christian women in medieval/ Renaissance Europe, Jewish women often worked with their husbands, running family businesses. However,

more frequently than other women, Jewish women came to be the major family breadwinner. As the study of Torah and the commentaries were the most honored occupations for Jewish men, some men spent virtually all their lives in study. Their wives freed them from the necessity of earning a living by becoming the economic provider as well as doing the domestic chores necessary for taking care of the family.[18]

Widows took over running the family businesses in order to be able to care for their children. Perhaps the most memorable of these family providers was one Gluckel of Hameln. Gluckel was unique because she wrote the only known autobiography of a Jewish woman in medieval/Renaissance Europe. She described, in a lively way, what it was like to be a middle class Jewish woman. Gluckel was altogether a remarkable person. Married at 14; she had 14 children; she was 44 when her husband died. For the next 10 years she worked at the family business, buying and selling seed pearls at fairs. Her memoirs were mostly about everyday events—the births of her children, their marriages, her husband's and her business dealings and personal sorrows. However, much of the

---

[13]This language is quite commonly called Yiddish—a mixture of middle German, Hebrew and other languages spoken by many European Jews.

[14]Sondra Henry and Emily Taitz, *Written Out of History* (New York: Bloch Publishing Co., 1978), p. 92-100.

[15]*Ibid.*, p. 115.

[16]*Ibid.*, p. 128.

[17]*Ibid.*, p. 132-133.

[18]Leo Jung, ed. *The Jewish Library, Vol. 3: Woman* (London: The Soncino Press, 1970), p. 42-43.

special world of European Jewish life was revealed in her writings. These excerpts from her book give some feeling of the life of this ordinary, yet unusual woman. Gluckel began her memoirs:

"In my great grief and for my heart's ease I begin this book the year of Creation 5451[19] [1690-91]—God soon rejoice us and send us His redeemer! I began writing it, dear children, upon the death of your good father, in the hope of distracting my soul from the burdens laid upon it, and the bitter thought that we have lost our faithful shepherd. In this way I have managed to live through many wakeful nights, and springing from my bed shortened the sleepless hours."

Gluckel's early memoirs reveal the special problems and sufferings of medieval/Renaissance Jews. Notice not only the prejudice against the Jews but how they help each other when in trouble:

"Before I was three years old, the German Jews, I am told were all driven out of Hamburg. Thereupon they settled in Altona which belonged to the king of Denmark, who readily gave them letters of protection. This city of Altona lies barely a quarter of an hour from Hamburg.

"About twenty-five Jewish families were previously settled in Altona, where we had our synagogue and cemetery. After we newcomers had remained there for some time, we finally succeeded with great difficulty in persuading the authorities of Hamburg to grant passes to Altona Jews, so we might enter and do business in that city. Such a pass was valid for four weeks, it was issued by the burgomaster and cost one ducat; when it expired

Jewish matron carrying a goose—the circle on her cloak was a common medieval requirement for Jews, meant to separate them from Christians.

another had to be procured in its stead. However, if you got to know the burgomaster or his officials, the old pass might be renewed for a second four weeks.

"This meant, God knows, a great hardship for our people, for all their business lay in Hamburg. Naturally, many a poor and needy wretch would try to slip into the city without a pass. If the officials caught him, he was thrust into prison, and then it cost all of us money and trouble to get him out again. In the early dawn, as soon as our folks were out of

---

[19]Date of the Jewish calendar which is a lunar calendar based on the date set for creation.

synagogue, they went down to Hamburg, and towards evening, when the gates were closed they came to Altona. Coming home, our poor folks often took their life in their hands because of the hatred for the Jews rife among the dockhands, soldiers and others of the meaner classes. The good wife, sitting home, often thanked God when her husband turned up safe and sound."

Later Gluckel's family and other Jews were allowed to return to Hamburg and her family arranged for her marriage when she was 14. Gluckel described her reaction to the start of her marred life:

"My father had me betrothed when I was a girl of barely 12, and less than two years later I married...Immediately afterwards my parents returned home and left me—I was a child of scarcely 14—alone with strangers in a strange world. That it did not go hard with me I owed to my new parents who made my life a joy. Both dear and godly souls, they cared after me better than I deserved. What a man he was, my father-in-law, like one of God's angels!

"Hameln, everyone knows what it is compared to Hamburg; taken by itself, it is a dull shabby hole. And there I was—a carefree child whisked in the flush of youth from parents, friends and everyone I knew, from a city like Hamburg plump into a back-country town where lived only two Jews."

As time went on Gluckel became her husband's business adviser and assistant:

"I was about twenty-five years old. My blessed husband worked manfully at his business, and although I was still young, I too did my share. Not that I mean to boast, but my husband took

advice from no one else, and did nothing without our talking it over together."

Gluckel was also occupied with numerous pregnancies and concerns of running a large family.

"...When my time was on me, the ever-faithful God so graciously lent me His aid, I gave birth almost without pain or effort, as though the child fell of its own will.

"It was a lovely, well-built child, but it came down at once with the selfsame fever as mine. Though we summoned doctors and every mortal aid, it proved of no avail. The child suffered fourteen days, and then God took back his share and left us ours, a bit of martyred clay. And me He left, a mother brought to bed—without her babe.

"...Thereafter I gave birth to my daughter Hendelchen, and two years later my son Samuel, then my son Moses, my daughter Freudchen, and my daughter Miriam. The two youngest barely knew their father.

"What indeed, shall I write of the gaps between times? Every two years I had a baby, I was tormented with worries as everyone is with a little house full of children, God be with them! and I thought myself more heavily burdened than anyone else in the world and that no one suffered from their children as much as I. Little I knew, poor fool, how fortunate I was when I seated my children like olive plants round about my table."

After her husband's death the widow Gluckel continued the family business while she raised her large family. Her children seemed to have been both a joy to her and a worry:

"My business prospered, I procured my wares from Holland, I bought nicely in Hamburg as well, and disposed of the goods in a

store of my own. I never spared myself, summer and winter I was out on my travels, and I ran about the city the livelong day.

"What is more, I maintained a lively trade in seed pearls. I bought them from all the Jews, selected and sorted them, and then resold them in towns where I knew they were in good demand.

"A whole year passed before the marriage of my son Moses fell due. Meanwhile reverses and troubles, falling partly to the lot of my children, overwhelmed me, and before and as always cost me great sums of money. But there is little need to write of it. They were my children and I forgive them all, both those who cost me much and those who cost me naught, for bringing me to my straitened circumstances.

"Moreover, I was still harrassed by a large business, for my credit had not suffered among either Jews or Gentiles, and I never cased to scrape and scurry. In the heat of summer and the rain and snow of winter I betook me to the fairs, and all day long I stood in my store."

Gluckel finally decided to marry again. This second marriage turned out disastrously as her husband lost both her savings and the business through bankruptcy. After her second husband's death, Gluckel reluctantly went to live with a daughter and her husband:

"Once when I was sick my son-in-law Moses visited me and said to me, I must dwell with him. He wanted to give me a room on the ground floor of his house, to save me climbing stairs. But I refused his offer, as I had many reasons for wishing never to live with my children.

"However, as things went, I could hold out no longer. So I finally yielded to what I had so long refused, and moved into he home of my son-in-law Moses Krumback...

"My son-in-law and my Daughter—long may they live!—and their children—God be with them!—were well contented with me.

"Shall I write you of how they treated me? There would be too much to tell. May the Father of goodness reward them! They paid me all the honors in the world. The best of everything was placed on my plate, more than I wanted or deserved, and I fear lest God count these bounties against my merits, which, alas, are few enough..."[20]

Gluckel, then, represents a strong and capable medieval woman. The fact of her being a member of a minority group may have strengthened these good qualities. It was necessary for Gluckel to overcome personal adversities, religious persecution and the restrictions felt as a Jew. Her memoirs reveal that she did so with rare resourcefulness and belief in her God.

[20]Marvin Lowenthal, tr. *The Memoirs of Gluckel of Hameln* (New York: Schocken Books, 1977), Book I, p. 1, 6-7, 8-9; Book II p. 23, 25; Book III p. 40; Book IV p. 142; Book V p. 179; Book VI p. 224; Book VII p. 265.

Points to Consider

1. List a few of the disabilities that affected all Jews in medieval/Renaissance Europe.

   List some special disabilities that affected only Jewish women.

   One commentator points out that in some ways Jewish women had a double burden in medieval/Renaissance times: They were not equals of Jewish men within Judaism, yet they suffered equally by being members of a persecuted minority.[21] In what specific ways might her comment seem correct?

   From your reading about Christian women in medieval times, what were some ways that Christian women were treated unequally with men within the Christian religion?

2. Although Jewish women may have suffered a double burden, the very fact of their being members of a persecuted minority forced Jewish women into open roles. Explain how the following factors might have created special opportunities for women:

   A. The poverty of most medieval and Renaissance Jews—caused in part by restrictions against owning land and entering certain occupations.

   B. The strong emphasis on male scholarship.

3. What may have made it possible for various exceptional women such as Perna of Fano, Devora Ascarelli and Rebecca Tiktiner to have succeeded in occupations dominated by men?

4. Why do you think Jewish women came to be lenders (particularly of small loans) to Christian women?

5. How would you describe Gluckel of Hameln in each of these roles:

   As wife?

   As mother?

   As business woman?

   As Jewish woman?

   What is your over-all impression of her as a person?

6. From these excerpts, what things seem to have been the most difficult about Gluckel's life? What the happiest? Do these sorrows and joys seem typical of medieval life? In what ways might they be the same if Gluckel lived now?

---

[21]Aviva Cantor Zuckoff, "The Oppression of the Jewish Woman," *Response Magazine*, Vol. 7 (Summer, 1973), p. 47-54.

C. European Women Tried as Witches
Victims of a Mania or Deep Social Injustice?

Introduction

The era from about 1350-1650 was noted for its obsession with witchcraft and witches. Historians disagree as to the reasons for this obsession. This was a period of great disruption within European society—when people's lives seemed threatened by instability and change. Perhaps this sort of atmosphere breeds the need to find a cause for troubles, to find scapegoats or victims to blame for disasters. A few of the disruptions and changes in late medieval/Renaissance times are suggested here:

- The Roman Catholic Church was increasingly challenged as the single voice of the Christian faith in Western Europe. During the Protestant Reformation of the 1600's this unity ended.

- The plague of the Black Death was epidemic in the 14th century and continued to reappear until the 18th century.

- Frequent wars between new nations, often over religious issues, brought widespread death and suffering.

- Following the epidemic of the Black Death in the 14th century, there was a movement of population from the country to the cities.

- This was a period of transition. Medieval values of a life of faith were being replaced by an age of science.

Whatever the basic cause of the witchcraft obsessions, the reality of the widespread nature of this obsession cannot be denied.

"Conservative estimates say 500,000 people were condemned to death for the crime of practicing witchcraft in Europe between the 14th and 17th centuries; other estimates are as high as several million. At least 80 percent of

those tried and condemned were women.'"[1]

- Did these witchcraft trials take place in ancient times and in remote parts of the world?

  No, these particular trials took place principally in Europe, a few in the Americas. Most occurred in the period of European history called the Renaissance, the great "rebirth" of art and science.

- Were the trials restricted to a particular area of Europe . . . only in Spain of the Inquisition or Switzerland of Calvinism?

  No, they occurred in England, Scotland, France, Spain, Switzerland, Germany, Italy . . . in isolated villages and in metropolitan towns and cities.

- Were those accusations and trials only a passing phase—a craze or hysterical outburst of a particular time of unrest?

  No, these witchcraft trials continued on and off, in various places in Western Europe, for over three hundred years.

- Was it only the Roman Catholic Church and their Inquisition that persecuted witches?

  No, Protestant leaders such as John Knox and Martin Luther, would continue the notion that witchcraft was practiced, especially by women, and that it was a heresy. Protestant Kings and Queens such as Henry VIII, Elizabeth I and James I of England passed laws condemning witchcraft. Therefore, witch trials and executions took place in both Catholic and Protestant parts of Europe.

- Were the trials conducted in secret with church or state authorities using medieval castles to hide away the accused and cover the executions?

No, the witchcraft trials were frequently conducted openly. The executions which usually followed were considered entertaining spectacles by the public. These executions were advertised and attracted large crowds of spectators. In England, those condemned to death died by hanging; on the continent the method of execution was usually burning at the stake.

★ ★ ★ ★ ★ ★

The following chapter will explore the phenomena of the European witchcraft trials from the point of view of women's history. The literature on the European witchcraft is vast; many historians have suggested various causes for the terrible fear of witches that led to these trials. Others have theorized the reasons women became the major target for the accusations of practicing witchcraft. As it is the aim of this book to present women's concerns in medieval and Renaissance life, the first part of this chapter will deal primarily with possible reasons why women were the major victims of witchcraft accusations. The second part of the chapter uses excerpts from various witchcraft records that tell the accusations and tortures used upon women during the trials. This second section includes trial records, broadsides advertising the executions of witches, a popular ballad about witches and the arguments of people who fought against the witch trials.

---

[1]William Monter, "The Historiography of European Witchcraft: Progress and Prospects," *Journal of Interdisciplinary History,* Vol. II (1972), p. 450.

Three terms—magic, sorcery and witches—are used frequently in this chapter. The following definitions will clarify these terms.

MAGIC:

A viewpoint that sees people as the central factor in the universe and everything in nature relating and being relevant to human's lives. In the magical view some people have powers to interpret nature's signs: They can foretell the future, control nature as well as the health, even life and death, of individuals. "High magic" may be involved in such philosophical pursuits as alchemy (gold-making) or astrology. "Low magic" involves attempts to get immediate results such as harming someone by sticking a pin in their image.

SCORCERY:

Use of primarily low magic techniques—such as spells, incantations and herbs— achieves immediate results such as rainfall, harm to individuals or cures for the sick.

WITCHES:

The definition varies from culture to culture but in medieval/ Renaissance Europe came to mean a Christian person who has rejected Christianity and worships the devil—thus a heretic or one who has fallen away from orthodox Christian belief. Witches also used witchcraft or sorcery to do harm to people. They were thought to be able to bring storms, kill animals, and human beings. European witchcraft also came to imply that the witch had the help of demons and the devil in her/his use of sorcery.[2]

★ ★ ★ ★ ★ ★

Women As Accused Witches

Belief in the power of magic and sorcery date from very ancient, prehistoric times. Classical folklore includes numerous ideas of the existence of female witches who could do harm by casting spells or using herbal poisons. In prehistoric times women may have been responsible for most food gathering and may have developed techniques of planting food for later harvesting. As the usual gatherers and gardeners, women had opportunities to learn about and experiment with the properties of plants.

These experiments led to the discovery of herbs and other plants and minerals that were medically useful in curing illness. Discoveries were also made of materials which were narcotic, hallucinogenic and even poisonous. Knowing the properties of plants and minerals, women could gain great power to cure—or to do harm. Later, in Roman and medieval times, some of these women were accused of being poisoners. Livia, widow of the

---

[2]For more complete definitions, see: Jeffrey Burton Russell, *Witchcraft in the Middle Ages* (Ithaca, NY: Cornell University Press, 1972), p. 3-26.

Roman Emperor Augustus, was thought to have plotted with a witch, Martina. Livia may have had Martina poison a rival of her son, Emperor Tiberius. So called wise women who knew the curative powers of ointments and herbs were traditionally consulted.

Another possible source for the idea that women were particularly prone to the practice of witchcraft might have been ancient religious beliefs. Some ancient religions, such as those of Isis and Ashera, emphasized the importance of fertility. These religions often held women in awe for their role of life giver. Statuary idols of pregnant women were objects of worship and believed to have magical properties. These ancient fertility religions, with their emphasis on female gods and pregnant female statuary as magical objects, may have led to the folklore idea that some women had special, even frightening, supernatural powers.

Women were frequently thought to have special powers since ancient times. Because of their importance in ancient fertility religions and their knowledge of the properties of plants and minerals, they were often thought to have the ability to use techniques of magic and sorcery. In addition to these ideas, was the ancient European folklore that described groups of night-flying female cannibals or strigae. By tradition these females were pictured as evil sorcerors casting malicious spells.[3] Therefore, another possible reason for women being special targets of later witchhunts was their association with ancient magical powers.

Belief in these special powers of women cannot fully explain the extent of the fear of women as witches which obsessed Europeans at the height of the witch hunt

Women as witches bringing hailstorm.

manias. In European witchcraft trials before the 1400's, about as many men as women were tried on charges relating to practicing forms of magic.[4] So, although women might have been associated with sorcery in the past, men were also accused of practicing sorcery in early medieval times as frequently as women.

One cause of the growing fear of sorcery and in particular women's involvement might have been related to the Roman Catholic Church's attitude toward witchcraft. The early

[3]E. William Monter, *Witchcraft in France & Switzerland* (Ithaca: Cornell University Press, 1976), p. 17.

[4]Richard Kieckhefer, *European Witch Trials* (Berkeley: University of California Press, 1976, p. 1-10.

Church took an interest in magic—usually condemning it as pagan belief. In the 10th century, a Church pronouncement was written on the evils of practicing sorcery. This pronouncement was believed by medieval people to be an early canon (Church law) and was frequently quoted (in various versions) in medieval times. Even though this "canon Episcopi" may not have actually been official Church doctrine, it provides a glimpse of what probably were rather common, early medieval witchcraft beliefs. Because the canon was often repeated, it seems to indicate an early fear of witchcraft especially as related to women, present long before the waves of mania from 1350-1650 A.D.

The pronouncement read:

"Bishops and their officials must labor with all their strength to uproot thoroughly from their parishes the evil art of sorcery and malefice [witches] invented by the devil, and if they find a man or woman follower of this wickedness to eject them foully disgraced from their parishes...It is also not to be omitted that some wicked women perverted by the devil seduced by illusions and phantasms of demons, believe and profess themselves, in the hours of night to ride upon certain beasts with Diana, the goddess of the pagans, and an innumerable multitude of women, and in the silence of the dead of night so traverse great spaces of earth, and to obey her commands as of their mistress, and to be summoned to her service on certain nights."[5]

In looking over this frequently quoted directive to church officials, note these specific aspects of the canon:

- Although the "canon Episcopi" first mentions both men and women as possible sorcerors or "malefice" (witches), the major portion elaborates on the special acts of women.

- Women are not yet accused of devil worship, as in later accusations, but here they are seen as perverted by the devil into belief in the pagan cult of Diana—the classical female God of the moon and forest.

- The canon declares that these women believe that they can travel great distances (by flying through the air, perhaps) and that there are a multitude of these women believers. The women are not actually accused of being able to fly, for example, but only that they believe they can.

Their offense, then, is belief in the pagan cult of Diana. Their punishment is exile from the community.

Even though these women were not declared devil worshippers, heretics or witches, some elements of later accusations are present in the early canon. Night meetings, traveling great distances riding on beasts and association with the devil would be common aspects of later witch accusations. Although both men and women were tried for sorcery, this early directive emphasized women's acts as especially wicked.

By the 14th century, the type of declarations against women as witches was changing. Diana now was only rarely seen as the cult object of witches' worship. These accused witches of the 14th century

---

[5]Russell, *Witchcraft.* p. 76.

121

were said to worship Satan or the devil. Various fairies, elves and magical folklore characters were now demons pictured in partnership with the devil. The later medieval witch was no longer seen as an unconverted believer in a pagan god, but as a heretic—the worst of sinners—a Christian who had sold out to the devil.[6] As will be seen, changes in medieval society may have contributed to the growing fear that women especially were capable of heresy or Satan worship and, therefore, were dangerous witches.

Two of the changes of the 12th century that led to accusations against women seemed highly favorable for women at first. One of these changes was the notion of courtly love that came into fashion at that time. The doctrine of courtly love declared that a knight should worship a lady, as an object of his adoration. Although the knight could declare his love through poems and songs written in her honor, the lady would remain beyond his marriageable reach. According to this doctrine, the perfect lovers would be the lady—a married woman—and an adoring knight.

The second development during the medieval period that also seemed to enhance the image of women, was the growing importance of the Virgin Mary, Mother of Jesus, as an object of worship by medieval Christians. This popular worship of Mary has been called the "cult of the Virgin." The cult of the Virgin viewed Mary as a loving mother willing to intervene with God for her "children."

Both or these developments, the ideas of courtly love and the cult of the Virgin, probably improved the status of some medieval women. Courtly love may have changed the view of medieval ladies as mere mothers. The lady, according to the

One artist's view of the courtly love tradition

doctrine of courtly love, was a valued object of adoration. The cult of the Virgin declared that some women were capable of selfless, tender mother love and saintly behavior. However, by creating these two specific ideal types of women models, an opposite—the idea of an evil type of woman was reinforced. This woman was the temptress Eve, evil and sexually depraved.[7] Though the Church declared Mary an ideal of womankind, at the same time it warned believers of women like Eve

---

[6]*Ibid.*, p. 101.

[7]For a more complete discussion on these two opposing views of medieval women see: E. William Monter, "The Pedestal and the Stake: Courtly Love and Witchcraft," Renate Bridenthal and Claudia Koonz, eds, *Becoming Visible: Women in European History* (Boston: Houghton Mifflin Co., 1977), p. 119-135.

Also: Russell, *Witchcraft in the Middle Ages,* p. 278-279.

who had lost paradise by her temptation of Adam. Furthermore, the doctrine of courtly love created a pedestal for the lady as a creature to be worshipped, while it permitted medieval knights to view peasant girls and women as fair game for their physical attention—even rape.

In both these medieval doctrines sexual contacts were suspect. In courtly love the woman was married and supposedly beyond her lover sexually. Though Mary was betrothed (engaged) to Joseph, she was declared to have been a virgin and sexually pure upon conceiving Jesus. These two views of the ideal woman might not improve the status of ordinary medieval women very much. As normal wives, mothers and sexual lovers, they could never attain the ideal. Accusations against medieval witches frequently included charges that the woman-witch had sexual intercourse with the devil. These accusations and women's confessions (usually extracted under terrible torture) were full of lurid sexual details. It seemed that the accused medieval witch became the direct opposite of the ideal medieval woman. Unlike the lady or the Virgin, a witch was sexually insatiable, even having intercourse with the devil himself. The witch was not thought to be a lady. One frequent accusation was that she kissed the devil's tail. She also was not a loving Virgin-mother. Another frequent accusation was that she killed and ate babies. Medieval people created ideals of womankind that were almost impossible for a human woman to attain. In doing so, they also created an image of the evil woman—sexually depraved, cruel and destructive—the heretic witch.

There are literally hundreds of trial records from various times and places in both Protestant and Catholic Europe in which women are

A woman being seduced by the devil

accused of sexual activities with demons or with Satan.

Two early examples from 14th century Italy seem mild in comparison to the next detailed confession of a 15th century woman accused of witchcraft.

"...An old woman named Gabrina Alletti who came from a relatively prosperous family in the village of San Prospero in Emilia, was brought to trial at Reggio in July, 1375. She had taught a number of other women how to sacrifice to the Devil. One of them alleged that Gabrina had instructed her to go out at night, take off her clothes, and kneel nude, looking up at the largest star in heaven (evidently an illusion to Satan's identity with Lucifer), crying out 'I adore thee, o

great Devil.' In this, one of the first clear witch cases in Italy, Gabrina was condemned to be branded and to have her tongue cut out.

"A woman named Maria was tortured in Florence, Italy, about 1375: she was alleged to have placed candles round a dish in the nude making magical signs."[8]

Besides these accusations of worshipping the devil, harsher crimes were attributed to a French woman of the 15th century. This Antonia, "confessed" to a common list of offenses including the eating of babies.

"In 1477 in the Savoyard town of Villars-Chabod, a woman called Antonia stubbornly refused to confess what the inquisitor Stephan Hudonodi demanded that she admit. After more than a month, the imprisonment and torture to which she was subjected broke her resistance, and at last she gave a lengthy confession...

[According to her confession:] "About eleven years earlier, one Massetus Garini found her in a state of sorrow and discontent and discovered that she had fallen into financial embarrassment. He told her that she could solve her problems by going with him to a certain friend. Reluctantly she left her home with him one evening. Massetus introduced her to a demon named Robinet, and said that he was the master of the group. He explained that to obtain her desires she would have to pay homage to this demon by denying God, the Catholic faith, and the Blessed Virgin, and taking Robinet as her lord and master. She hesitated. Robinet addressed her in a barely intelligible voice, promising her gold, silver, and

other good things; others in attendance likewise encouraged her. Then she consented, kissed the demon's foot, received a 'sign' on her left little finger (which was deadened ever afterward), and trampled and broke a wooden crucifix. The demon gave her a purse full of gold and silver and a magic stick. When she rubbed the stick and recited an appropriate incantation, the stick would transport her through the air to the synagogue (or meeting). After further feasting and dancing, the members of the sect paid homage to the demon—who by now had changed into the form of a black dog—by kissing him on the tail. Then the demon cried out 'Meclet! Meclet!' and the fire was put out, whereupon the participants in the festivity gave themselves over to each other sexually. When the meeting was over Antonia went home, only to find that the purse she thought was filled with gold and silver was in fact empty. In further confessions she told of the activities she engaged in as a member of the sect...further meetings, consumption of human infants, manufacture of magic powders from the bones and intestines of these babies, use of such powders to inflict illness and death on men and animals..."[9]

Women, then, as witches were seen as the evil opposite of the ideal of feminine virtue. The era from 1450-1700 seems to have been a time of controversy concerning women's nature. While many men defended women, there were also,

[8]Russell, *Witchcraft in the Middle Ages*, p. 209-210.

[9]Kieckhefer, *European Witch Trials*, p. 25-26.

attitudes of misogyny (hatred and fear of women) in theology and literature.[10] This misogyny helped increase belief in the evil doings of "witches" and may partly explain why the majority tried and executed for witchcraft were women.

The following excerpts are from the most renowned work written about witchcraft during this period. It was written in 1486 by two Inquisitors (Catholic church investigators of heresy), Heinrich Kramer and Jacob Sprenger. Called the *Malleus Maleficarum* or *Hammer of Witches,* it became the most consulted encyclopedia of witch hunting techniques of the 1700's.[11] Kramer and Sprenger reflect this misogyny in these excerpts from the *Hammer of Witches.* They also frequently mentioned sexual misconduct on the part of witches. Just before Kramer and Sprenger wrote the *Hammer of Witches* they were responsible for bringing fifty people to trial on charges of witchcraft. All but two were women.[12]

"Why it is that Women are chiefly addicted to Evil Superstitions.

"Now the wickedness of women is spoken of in Ecclesiasticus XXV (in the Apocrypha[13] of the Bible): There is no head above the head of a serpent: and there is no wrath above the wrath of a woman. I had rather dwell with a lion and a dragon than to keep house with a wicked woman. And among much which in that place precedes and follows about a wicked woman, he concludes: All wickedness is but little to the wickedness of a woman. What else is woman but a foe to friendship, an unescapable punishment, a necessary evil, a natural temptation, a desirable calamity, a domestic danger, a delectable detriment, an evil of nature, painted with fair color!...

"The second reason is that women are naturally more impressionable and more ready to receive the influence of a disembodied spirit; and that when they use this quality well they are very good, but when they use it ill they are very evil.

"The third reason is that they have slippery tongues, and are unable to conceal from their fellow-women those things which by evil arts they know; and, since they are weak, they find an easy and secret manner of vindicating themselves by witchcraft...

"It should be noted that there was a defect in the formation of the first woman, since she was formed from a bent rib, that is, a rib of the breast, which is bent as it were in a contrary direction to a man. And since through this defect she is an imperfect animal, she always deceives.

"Therefore a wicked woman is by her nature quicker to waver in her faith which is the root of witchcraft."[14]

---

[10]See: Ruth Kelso, *Doctrine for the Lady of the Renaissance* (Urbana, IL: University of Illinois Press, 1956), p. 5-37; Monter, *Witchcraft,* p. 20-26.

[11]Alan C. Kors and Edward Peters, eds, *Witchcraft in Europe 110-1700* (Philadelphia: University of Pennsylvania Press, 1972), Introduction.

[12]Monter, *Witchcraft,* p. 26.

[13]Apocrypha: Commonly used to mean the fourteen books of the Bible excluded from the authorized version as nonauthentic.

[14]Kors and Peters, *Witchcraft* in Europe, p. 114-121.

Misogyny, such as that of the Inquisitors Kramer and Sprenger, may help to explain why women were particularly singled out as witches. Additional causes have been suggested by modern scholars. For example, one modern investigator, Jeffrey Russell, has suggested that a larger proportion of women than men supported various forms of heresy. They may have done so as a rebellion against the medieval social institutions that frequently placed them in an inferior position. Perhaps some women did turn to witchcraft or heresies against the Church as a way to gain a kind of power and fearsome respect.

Another scholar, Josiah Russell, suggested that in c. 1450 there was a shift from European witchcraft trials which involved almost equal numbers of men and women, to trials in which the accused were mostly or entirely women. Russell points out that population studies of medieval Europe suggest that by the 15th century there were considerably more women than men. Since the tendency is for women to outlive men, this might partly explain the presence of a large group of elderly widowed women.[15] Additionally, historian Eric Midelfort described changing marriage patterns in the 15th century showing people marrying later or not at all. In late medieval times, cities and towns grew in importance. Younger family members may have left the country for work in the cities, leaving elderly women relatives alone in the villages. In medieval society, women of all ages were expected to be under the authority of men (fathers, husbands or grown sons). Russell and Midelfort speculate that these single, often elderly women were left alone without family to take an interest in their welfare. These women, thus, became easy and safe targets for witchcraft accusations.[16]

In summary, there were a number of reasons for women's vulnerability to accusations of practicing witchcraft:

- Women were long associated with possessing special magical powers.

- Both the Roman Catholic Church and the later Protestant Churches often pictured women as more gullible, therefore more likely, to stray into heresies.

- The ideals of medieval womankind—the courtly Lady and the Virgin Mother—were hard for ordinary women to copy. These ideals of perfection implied their opposite—the Witch.

- Misogyny (hatred of women) was one characteristic of society in late medieval and early Renaissance times. This created an atmosphere that might condone or even approve violence directed toward women.

- Modern research seems to indicate that there may have been a large group of single or widowed older women who, because of their lack of family protection, were easy, safe targets for accusations as witches.

---

[15]Russell, p. 281. Population information from Josiah Cox Russell, *British Medieval Population* (Albuquerque: University of New Mexico Press, 1948), p. 202. Josiah Russell's study seems to indicate that more men than women died in plagues—especially The Black Death of the 14th century.

[16]H.C. Erik Midelfort, *Witchhunting in Southwestern Germany 1562-1684* (Stanford: Stanford University Press, 1972), p. 184-185.

Points to Consider

1. Why were women from very ancient times often associated with having special powers?

   How might their roles as gatherers or gardeners have contributed to the later idea that they were witches?

2. Before about 1450, as many men as women were accused of using sorcery or witchcraft in European courts. Explain why the following changes that occurred in medieval thinking might have contributed to a rise of witchcraft accusations.

- Witchcraft was looked at as heresy by the Church after about 1450—before it was seen as a form of paganism.

- The development of the ideal of courtly love and the cult of the Virgin.

- Misogyny.

- Changes in population, sex ratios of men to women and changes in marriage patterns.

3. After reading this essay, what do you think might have been the reasons for the witch trials?

   Why do you think women were the major targets?

   After you read the second part of the essay, ask yourself whether your opinion changed about the causes of the witchcraft mania with women as the main victims.

4. In medieval times there was a dual view of women—the idea of the Virgin Mother and the evil of Eve. Do you think women are still divided into these two images of either good or bad women?

   Is there a double standard for men?

5. Why do you think that various medieval saints were frequently in some danger of being accused of being witches?

   Might there be several reasons? (Remember that St. Catherine of Siena and St. Teresa of Avila were under some suspicion and St. Joan of Arc was condemned to death for witchcraft.)

Records of the Witchcraft Era

There is an abundance of materials on the European witchcraft obsession. The following excerpts represent only a few documents out of thousands. They were selected as representative of the records that remain from the trials. These materials also illustrate aspects of the history of medieval and Renaissance women in the era of witchcraft trials.

- The first excerpt suggests that the printing press may have increased popular interest in witchcraft trials.

- The second suggests that the use of torture may have contributed in large number to confessions of witchcraft.

- The third section suggests that there were several men who forcefully argued against the witchcraft trials even at the height of the witch manias.

IOAN PRENTIS
& hir Bid

JACK

GILL

Broadside of the execution of the Chelmsford witches.

Publicizing the Trials and Executions

The printing press was invented and first used in Germany in the 15th century. This made possible a much cheaper method of reproducing books. The invention of the printing press is considered a cause of the Renaissance because scientific knowledge, as well as classical literature, could be widely distributed. However, although the new printing was used for many worthy projects such as printing the Bible and the classics, it also could be used for distributing sensational stories, or even pornography. The following ballad is typical of the printed materials about witchcraft trials. Ballads, broadsides (single sheets) and pamphlets were quickly written, cheaply printed and sold to the public to advertise witchcraft trials and executions. These advertisements were often gruesomely illustrated. One historian comments that, *"The sheets were sold for a half-penny or less in England, and such was the enthusiasm and delight displayed by those eager hands which purchased them, that today copies of all but a few have been completely worn out or destroyed."*[1]

This excerpt from a printed ballad tells about the third Chelmsford Trial in England that took place in 1589. Three accused of witchcraft, Joan Coney, Joan Upney and Joan Prentice died by hanging, two hours after they were pronounced guilty. Note of what the witches were accused and by whom.

---

[1]Peter Haining, ed., *The Witchcraft Papers* (London: Robert Hale & Co., 1974), p. 72.

128

A New Ballad of the Life and Deaths of
Three Witches Arraigned and Executed at Chelmsford
5 July 1589

List Christians all unto my Song
'Twill move your Hearts to Grace,
That Dreadful Witchcraft hath been done,
Of late about this place;
But Three that cried the Devil's Name
With those who did them follow,
Now to Justice are brought home
To swing upon our Gallow.

A vile long life they have run on
Regarding not their End,
Their Hearts still bent to cruelty
Not minding to Amends:
Men and cattle they Bewitched
No Peace they gave to Rest,
But yet, in turn the parts were switched
By Marks upon their Breasts.

As to the Story now to tell
The Truth I will Declare,
It was the Witches Children small
That they did not Beware;
For God into these Infants' Hearts
Did pour the Light of Reason,
And all against their Mothers spoke
Of Witchcraft and of Treason.

So listen Christians to my Song
The Hangman's swung his rope,
And on these Gallows hath been done
An end to Satan's Hope;
Give the News from Chelmsford Town
To all the world be spread,
A crew of Evil Witches have gone Down
Hang'd by the neck, all three are Dead.[2]

[2]Ibid., p. 73-75.

Torture and Witch Confessions

"June 17, arrested and imprisoned on suspicion of witchcraft, June 18, tortured, but did not confess. June 20 tortured, and 'confessed': June 28, her 'confession' read to her. June 30 "confession" confirmed and sentence pronounced: July 4, execution date announced: July 7, executed."

Trial of Anna Hansen, 1629[3]

The above trial record shows both the haste of many of these trials and the open use of torture as a method of gaining confessions. The following descriptions of witch accusations and trials are also typical of the kinds of confessions made by accused women after torture. The role of torture in extracting confessions of witchcraft is an important aspect of these trials. One historian of the trials in France and Italy in the 15th century observed that, *"the extent of the confessions appears to have been directly proportional to the length of torture."*[4]

This historian, Richard Kieckhefer, described one such confession of a women named Antonia whose trial was discussed earlier.

". . . A Savoyard court apprehended a woman named Antonia in 1477. She denied under oath that she was guilty of 'heresy' (meaning in this case witchcraft). Asked if she knew why she had been detained, she said those who had seized her said it was for reasons of faith. She denied that she had ever been defamed as a witch, or fled to avoid arrest for witchcraft. Evidently she admitted some form of magic, but she insisted that she had never gone to diabolical assemblies, and denied knowledge of what witches did. The inquisitor gave her a formal threefold monition to tell the truth, over a period of three days. He interrogated her further, asking about quarrels she had had with various persons. The. . . [prosecutor] requested [a] sentence, which would lead to torture, providing the accused had no valid objections to this measure. Antonia pleaded only that she was innocent of witchcraft, but this was evidently not a legitimate objection. The woman was taken to the place of torture and raised on the strappado[5] three cubits from the floor, for about half an hour. She refused to confess, but asked for time to deliberate, and was taken down. Tortured again on the following day, she pleaded that if she were released from torture she would tell the truth. Yet it was only after a further day's deliberation that she broke down and confessed her engagement in diabolism [with the devil]."[6]

In 1652 a woman named Suzanne Gandry was tried for witchcraft at Roux near Paris, France. Even though old and perhaps confused, Suzanne Gandry seems to have held out against considerable torture— even recanting (taking back) one confession—before she finally confessed to the usual crimes of

---

[3]Hans Sebald, *Witchcraft: The Heritage of a Heresy* (New York: Elsevier, 1978) p. 33.

[4]Richard Kieckhefer, *European Witch Trials* (Berkeley: University of California Press, 1976), p. 89.

[5]A form of torture, tying the victim's wrists behind her back and then raising her by the wrists.

[6]Kieckhefer, *European Witch Trials*, p. 24.

devil worship. This excerpt is from the actual trial records. It describes the end of her trial when she was again tortured and forced to confess a second time; whereupon she was convicted and executed.

The Torture

"On this same day, being at the place of torture. This prisoner, [Suzanne Gandry] before being strapped down was [told] to maintain herself in her first confessions and to renounce her lover (the devil).

• *Said that she denies everything she has said and that she has no lover. Feeling herself being strapped down, says that she is not a witch, while struggling to cry. Asked why she fled outside the village of Rieux.*

• *Says that she cannot say it, that God and the Virgin Mary forbid her to, that she is not a witch. And upon being asked why she confessed to being one, said that she was forced to say it. Told that she was not forced that on the contrary she declared herself to be a witch without any threat.*

• *Says that she confessed it and that she is not a witch, and being a link stretched [on the rack] screams ceaselessly that she is not a witch, involving the name of Jesus and Our Lady of Grace not wanting to say any other thing.*

• *Asked if she did not confess that she had been a witch for twenty-six years.*

• *Says that she said it, that she retracts it, crying Jesus-Maria that she is not a witch.*

• *Asked if she did not make Philippe Cornie's horse die, as she confessed.*

• *Answers no, crying Jesus-Maria, that she is not a witch.*
The mark having been probed by the officer, in the presence of Doctor Bouchain, it was adjudged by the aforesaid doctor and officer truly to be the mark of the devil.

• *Being more tightly stretched upon the torture-rack, urged to maintain her confessions.*

• *Said that it was true that she is a witch and that she would maintain what she had said.*

• *Asked how long she has been in subjugation to the devil.*

• *Answers that it was twenty years ago that the devil appeared at her home in her lodgings in the form of a man dressed in a little cow-hide and black breeches.*

• *Interrogated as to what her lover was called.*

• *Says that she said Petit-Grignon [Little Devil] then, being taken down [from the rack] says upon interrogation that she is not a witch and that she can say nothing.*

• *Asked if her lover has had carnal copulation with her, and how many times.*

• *To that she did not answer anything; then, making believe that she was ill, not another word could be drawn from her.*

"As soon as she began to confess, she asked who was alongside of her, touching her, yet none of those present could see anyone there. And it was noticed that as soon as that was said, she no longer wanted to confess anything.

"Which is why she was returned to prison."

Verdict
July 9, 1652

"In the light of the interrogations, answers and investigations made into the charge against Suzanne Gandry, coupled with her confessions, from which it would appear that she has always been ill-reputed for being stained with the crime of witchcraft, and seeing that she took flight and sought refuge in this city of Valenciennes, out of fear of being apprehended by the law for this matter; seeing how her close family were also stained with the same crime, and the perpetrators executed; seeing by her own confessions that she is said to have made a pact with the devil...

"For expiation of which the advice of the under-signed is that the office of Rieux can legitimately condemn the aforesaid Suzanne Gandry to death, tying her to a gallows and strangling her to death, then burning her body and burying it there in the environs of the woods.

"At Valenciennes, the 9th of July, 1652. To each [member of the Court] 4 livres, 16 sous....And for the trip of the aforementioned Roux, including an escort of one soldier 30 livres."[7]

Reginald Scot: Sanity in Answer to Mania

In 1584 soon after the famous English St. Osyth witch trials, an English country gentleman, Reginald Scot, wrote a book called, *Discoverie of Witchcraft*. By "Discoverie" Scot meant an uncovering or revealing of the stupidity of believing in witches' powers and he poured scorn on the

"Swimming a witch"—if the accused women floated she was guilty, if not she was proven innocent—but usually drowned.

witch hunters of his day.[8] These were astonishing opinions to express and have printed at the height of the English witch hunts. In fact, to publish such ideas was a courageous act as it might have led to accusations of witchcraft against Scot.[9]

In the following excerpts from his book, Reginald Scot reveals that the usual witch was none other than a harmless old woman—who may

[7]Alan C. Kors and Edward Peters, eds, *Witchcraft in Europe* (Philadelphia: University of Pennsylvania Press, 1972), p. 274-275.

[8]Edgar Peel and Pat Southern, *The Trials of the Lancashire Witches* (New York: Taplinger Publishing Co., 1969), p. 129.

[9]*Ibid.*, p. 129.

have looked or acted strangely because of her age and vulnerability rather than by evil doings. Notice that his observations of old, poor women being accused fits historians Russell and Midelfort's ideas of a population imbalance in late medieval times. Their theories are that old women outnumbered old men and that there were large numbers of single elderly women left behind in villages as population shifted to cities.

"Note how easily they [a woman accused of witchcraft] might be brought to confess that which they never did. They which are commonly accused of witchcraft are the least sufficient of all persons to speak for themselves, the extremity of their age giving them leave to dote, their poverty to. . .be full of imagination. . . .

"The poor old witch is commonly unlearned, unwarned, and unprovided of counsel and friendship. . .voice of judgement and discretion. She is daunted by authority, compelled by fear, deceived by ignorance and so brought to these absurd confessions. . . .One sort commonly said to be witches are women which are old, lame, blear-eyed, foul and full of wrinkles. Poor, sullen and superstitious creatures in whose drowsy minds the 'Devil' hath a fine seat. So as whatever mischief is brought to pass they are easily persuaded the same is done by themselves. These wretches are so odious to their neighbours and so feared that few dare offend them or deny them anything they ask—from this they come to think that they can do such things as are beyond the ability of human nature.

"They go from door to door for a potful of milk or potage without which they could hardly live. It happens sometimes that their expectations go unanswered as in course of time the witch becomes tedious to her neighbours. So sometimes she cursed one, then the other, until, as they all displease her, she curses master, wife, children and cattle.

"In time some of her neighbours fall sick, or their cattle die, and they suppose it to be the vengeance of witches. The witch, on the other hand, seeing one in every hundred of her curses take effect, is convinced that she herself has brought this misfortune to pass, and confesses it. So she, her accusers, and the justices, are all deceived."[10]

Scot died in 1599. James I, who became king of England at the death of Elizabeth I in 1603, published his *Demonology* that defended witchcraft trials and called for stronger laws against witches. Although he later had a change of heart, five women were executed in the nine years of his reign. In the preface to *Demonology,* he condemned Scot's book and when he became King of England ordered copies of it destroyed.[11] Still, slowly more reasonable voices spoke up against witchcraft trials and in defense of accused witches. For example, in the late 1600's, on the continent—the Frenchman Pierre Bayle and the Dutch pastor

---

[10]Quoted in: *Ibid.*, p. 130-131.

[11]*Ibid.*, p. 132.

BALTHASAR BEKKER,
der Heiligen Schrifft Doctor,
und Prediger zu Amsterdam.

Balthasar Bekker wrote forcefully
against witchcraft belief.

At the last English witchcraft trial
in 1712, an old woman named Jane
Weham, the accused witch, was
found guilty by the jury. However,
the skeptical judge questioned them
saying, ***"Do you really find her
guilty . . . for conversing with the
Devil in the shape of a cat?"***[12]
When the jury said yes—the judge
was forced to give her a death
sentence, but he then made sure
Jane Weham received a royal
pardon. The end of British witchcraft
persecutions came when an English
Bishop, Francis Hutchinson,
published an attack on witchcraft as
a total delusion.[13] Although laws
changed more slowly on the
continent, by the mid-1700's the
European witch mania was over.

Points to Consider

1. In the "Ballad of Chelmsford
   Witches," who gave evidence
   against women at their trials?

   How might you explain this?

2. Why might ballads, broadsides
   and other forms of advertising
   have increased the number of
   trials and lengthened the mania?

3. In the trial of Antonia, in what
   specific ways does her confession
   change under torture?

   Under what conditions did
   Suzanne Gandry confess?
   Recant? Confess again?

   Why might even the soldier in her
   escort have reason to support
   these trials? Do people seem to
   have been spectators at the trial
   and execution?

4. List some stereotypes of a witch
   (think of Halloween and ghost
   stories). In what ways does
   Reginald Scot's witch fit your
   description?

   Why do you suppose that the
   stereotyped witch figure was really
   the type of woman most often
   accused of witchcraft—old,
   widowed or alone, frequently poor
   and often with pet cats?

   Unlike Scotland and the
   Continent, torture was not used in
   England to force witches to
   confess (although such techniques
   as keeping the accused awake for
   several days were used). There
   were fewer convictions of witches
   in England than where torture was
   used. Why does Scot think some
   women confessed even though
   they were not tortured?

---

[12]*Ibid.*, p. 167.

[13]*Ibid.*, p. 167.

Witches were reported to be cannibals who ate infants.

How might these women have been brainwashed into confessing to these charges?

5. Can you think of other instances where societies have selected a vulnerable group of people on whom to project its fears and insecurities (scapegoating)?

6. *"[One of] the last officially recorded witch executions in Germany took place in 1749 in the Wurzburg diocese when a 71-year-old woman (a nun for 50 years) was carried, because she was too frail to walk, to her place of execution."*[14]

Why might even a nun have been accused of witchcraft practices?

Why do you think incidents such as this one might have led to people speaking up against witchcraft trials and putting an end to them?

[14]Hans Sebald, *Witchcraft: the Heritage of a Heresy* (New York: Elsevier, 1978), p. 49.

135

Group Exercise

Historians have long argued whether there really were large groups of people who were practicing witchcraft in the period of the witch hunts. Opinions vary greatly. In the 1920's, historian Margaret Murray wrote a famous book on witches claiming that many medieval/Renaissance people (mostly women) were witches or at least left-over pagans (believers in the "old religions")[1] However, she claimed that they were harmless women who were dissenters from Christianity. Another English writer of the same period, Montague Summers[2] claimed they really were witches—harmful and evil—and that witchcraft was still widely practiced in the 20th century. Still others have claimed that witchcraft was invented by the Inquisition to get rid of remaining believers in paganism and that it continued and was inflamed by the religious controversies and wars.[3] Others have called the trials a form of mass hysteria which literally hypnotically claimed people's minds.[4] In addition, there is a whole range of opinions from historians who believe that some medieval people practiced mild forms of "folk" or "low" magic, to those who suggest that lonely, old women might have tried using witchcraft against their village enemies.[5] Recently several women authors have suggested that the accusations and trials were entirely a result of misogyny—women-hating; a grotesque example of what these women authors see as women's traditionally powerless and inferior status. They claim the accused women were practicing folk medicine seen as heresy because men did not want women using this power as midwives or wise women.[6]

CITATIONS—

[1] Margaret Murray, *The Witch Cult in Western Europe* (Oxford: Oxford University Press, 1921).

[2] Montague Summers,*The History of Witchcraft and Demonology* (London, 1926).

[3] Hugh Trevor-Roper, *Religion, the Reformation and Social Change* (New York, 1968).

[4] See for example, Charles McKay, *Extraordinary Popular Delusions and The Madness of Crowds.* (London: Richard Benley, 1841 Reprinted New York: Harmony Books, 1980.) pp. 521-522.

[5] See such modern historians: Jeffrey Russell, *Witchcraft in the Middle Ages* (Ithaca: Cornell University Press, 1972); H.C. Erik Midelfort *Witchhunting in Southwestern Germany* (Stanford: Stanford University Press, 1972); E. William Monter *Witchcraft in France and Switzerland* (Ithaca: Cornell University Press, 1976); Hans Sebald, *Witchcraft The Heritage of a Heresy* (New York: Elsevier, 1978).

[6] Mary Daly, *Gyn/Ecology* (Boston: Beacon Press, 1978). Andrea Dworkin, *Woman Hating* (New York: E.P. Dutton, 1974).

★ ★ ★ ★ ★ ★

Think back over the evidence given in this chapter and then see what evidence supports each of these positions:

- Women might actually have been practicing witchcraft during medieval/Renaissance times. These witches probably belonged to cults of ancient religions.

- Witchcraft was invented by the Inquisition and other authorities and women's confessions meant nothing.

- Witchcraft was a way to attack women and keep them from practicing medicine such as midwifery, while acting as wise women of the village.

Which position seems most strongly supported by the historical evidence given here? Explain your choice.

Can you think of other possible answers to the puzzle of why women were the chief victims of the witchcraft mania?

Chapter 5
Education of Women in Medieval/Renaissance Europe

A. The Debate on Whether Women Could/Should Learn

There were basically two positions on women's education in the medieval and Renaissance periods. These were that:

- women were naturally intellectually inferior and, therefore, could not learn.

- women were capable of learning but their education should be confined to knowledge which would aid them to be good, pious wives or nuns.

These two positions were debated mostly by men. Often, these debates became widespread in countries in which women ruled. For example, there was an outpouring of books on the nature on women in France during one regency of Anne of Austria;[1] a similar abundance of books, pamphlets and tales about women came out during the reign of Elizabeth I of England.[2] The debate about women's ability to learn was usually based on two sources—the Bible and classical, pseudo (false) scientific writings.

The first position—that women were intellectually inferior and could not learn—had as a major obstacle to acceptance, the concept that men and women were moral equals as Christians. However, according to the view that women were inferior by nature, Eve's act of eating the apple from the tree of knowledge had brought a curse upon her and upon all women. Women's reasoning power thereafter, according to Tertulian, an early Christian writer,

---

[1]Ian Maclean, *Woman Triumphant: Feminism in French Literature 1610-1652* (Oxford: Clarendon, 1977), p. 27.

[2]Louis B. Wright, *Middle Class Culture in Elizabethan England* (Chapel Hill: University of North Carolina Press, 1935), p. 465-507.

was faulty and she became *"the door to the devil."*[3] With this view in mind, educating women could only increase their chances for wickedness. An extreme example of this position occurred in 16th century France when a woman was stoned for merely suggesting the idea of a school for girls.[4]

Another argument against education for women was put forth by the medieval philosopher, Thomas Aquinas (1225-1274), who based his views about women on Aristotle, (384-322 B.C.), the ancient Greek philosopher. Aristotle thought that women were an inferior sub-species of humans. According to Aristotle's pseudo-scientific views, women had higher temperatures, more teeth and were physically incomplete when compared to men.

Other false medical ideas accepted in the medieval period included the thought that a woman's womb was like an independent being, an animal inside her which interfered with her reasoning powers.[5] Aquinas combined all these ideas in his writings and arrived at the conclusion that women were incomplete when compared with men. They were not a part of the ordinary course of Nature (practer naturam) but instead Aquinas associated women with monsters of Nature.[6] A follower of Aquinas, Thomas de Via, Cardinal Cajetan (1469-1534), described women as always half asleep, or half virile.[7] Women, according to this theory, could learn but their abilities were limited when compared with those of men. This attitude toward women's faculties might be summarized by a 17th century Englishman writing about his daughter: *"Peggy is very backward...I doubt not but she will be scholar enough for a woman."*[8]

There was, however, the other side to the debate on women's education—that they were capable of learning but should only study as a way to increase their piety. As early as the 2nd century, the Christian leader Clement of Alexandria, pointed out in his *Paedagogus,* that the word of Christianity was meant for women as well as for men. Thus, the text of the New Testament (either heard or read) was as appropriate for them as for men.[9] St. Jerome (c. 342-420), while stressing the need for watchful and moral tutors for girls, wrote letters to his friend Laeta advising her to educate her daughter Paula. Paula was not to learn to play the lute or to dress in fancy clothes, but she should learn to read and write in the languages of Greek and Latin.[10] Afraid that Paula might be tempted by outside distractions, St. Jerome encouraged her to be educated within a convent. St. Augustine (354-430), another major early Church theologian, wrote that women had the same faculties of mind as men—memory, active intellect and will.[11]

---

[3]Ian MacLean, *The Renaissance Notion of Woman* (Cambridge: Cambridge University Press, 1980), p. 15.

[4]Edith Sichel, *Women and Men of the French Renaissance* (Port Washington, New York: Kennikat Presses, 1970), (1901), p. 20.

[5]Maclean, *Woman Triumphant,* p. 9.

[6]Maclean, *Renaissance Notion of Women,* p. 12.

[7]Quoted in *Ibid.,* p. 9.

[8]Myra Reynolds. *The Learned Lady in England 1650-1760* (Boston: Houghton Mifflin, 1950), p. 24.

[9]Maclean, *The Renaissance Notion of Women,* p. 20.

[10]Dorothy Gardiner, *English Girlhood at School* (London: Oxford University Press, 1929), p. 4-6.

[11]Maclean, *Renaissance Notion of Women,* p. 13.

These ideas formed the basis for the defense of women's education down to the Renaissance. However, as convents lessened as centers of learning in the Renaissance, an interest grew in educating women in secular (non-religious) schools or at courts not necessarily associated with the Church. There was a new and widespread feeling that women could learn even non-religious subjects. Among male writers of the Renaissance who encouraged women's education were Cornelius Agrippa, Juan Luis Vives, Desiderius Erasmus, Robert Ascham and, perhaps most famous, Thomas More of England. More raised his daughters, as well as his sons, to be intellectuals, and one daughter, Margaret Roper, was known throughout Europe for her wit and ability with languages. Thomas More expressed his attitude toward equal education as follows:

"Neither is there any difference at harvest time whether it was man or woman, that sowed first the corn; for both or them bear name of a reasonable creature equally whose nature reason only doth distinguish from brute beasts, and therefore I do not see why learning in like manner may not equally agree with both sexes; for by it, reason is cultivated, and (as a field) sowed with wholesome precepts, it bringeth forth excellent fruit."[12]

Yet, the emphasis in the writings of most or these men was still upon educating women's spiritual lives, though no longer as nuns. Louis XIV, for example, financed the dream of his morganatic wife, Madame de Maintenon, to build a school for girls based on the principles of Vives and More. While the school did not encourage women to become nuns, it did stress Christian virtues and duties for the future wife and mother. Novels, formal science and difficult theological theories were not part of curriculum.[13] Vives was asked by Catherine of Aragon to write a book of advice for her daughter, the future Mary I of England. He did so. It was entitled the *Christian Woman* and stressed the virtuousness of pious learning and submission to a husband's wishes.

"Nature has given unto man a noble, a high and a diligent mind to be busy and occupied abroad. To gain and to bring home to their wives and family, to rule them and their children and also all their household. And to the woman nature has given a fearful, a covetous and humble mind to be subject unto man."[14]

As one historian has pointed out however, Vives' advice "completely ignored" the fact that he was supposed to be writing for a future queen who would rule England.[15]

By the end of the Renaissance, the second side of the debate had generally been successful by those who agreed that women *could* learn. Still, there were fears about educating women, especially when the religious passions of the Protestant Reformation erupted. Would reading lead to more heresy, like the Lollard women of England? Or to less if the Ursaline nuns taught young women in strict convent schools? But basically the idea that

---

12Mary Agnes Cannon, *The Education of Women During the Renaissance* (Washington, D.C.: Catholic University, 1916), p. 99.

13H. C. Barnard, *Madame de Maintenon and Saint-Cyr* (London: A & C Black, 1934), p. 172.

14Quoted in Ruth Kelso, *Doctrine for the Lady of the Renaissance* (Urbana: University of Illinois Press, 1956), p. 17-18.

15*Ibid.*, p. 263.

This woman supervises her kitchen workers.

- Should resources of money be spent equally on women and men? Martin Luther wanted free schools for all children of all economic classes.[18]

- Should women be teachers? The Italian, Bruns, said, *"I allow women to learn, to teach never."*[19] Meanwhile, although the number of women teachers and governesses was beginning to grow, their numbers did not match those of male teachers. For example, in Lyon, France, in the years 1490-1560, there were only five women teachers out of a total of 87.[20]

By the 17th century, the issues of educating women had just begun to be discussed. Some issues are yet to be resolved as the controversy over how best to implement Title IX, the United States' law requiring equal education, shows.[21]

women, at least women of the upper classes, should be literate, if not too intellectual, was basically accepted.

There were other debates besides these two about women's education that have continued into the 20th century. By the late Renaissance, some of these were:

- Should schools be co-educational? Thomas More thought they should; others were horrified at the thought of the *"terrible dangers"* of mixing the sexes in schools.

- Should women be trained for politics, law, medicine and wider fields than merely the domestic one? John Case, the English scholar, thought so, *"If one is born free why should she obey?"*[16] Others, like Martin Luther, wanted training only so that women could learn how to raise children well.[17]

[16]Maclean, *Renaissance Notion of Women,* p. 60.

[17]Mary Cathcart Borer, *Willingly to School: A History of Women's Education* (London: Lutterworth, 1975), p. 70-71.

[18]*Ibid.,* p. 70.

[19]Quoted in, R. de Maulde la Claviere, *Women of the Renaissance* (New York: G. P. Putnam's Sons, 1900), p. 98.

[20]Natalie Zemon Davis, *Society and Culture in Early Modern France* (Stanford: Stanford University Press, 1975), p. 73.

[21]Title IX of the Education Amendments of 1972 says: "No person . . . shall, on the basis of sex, be excluded from participation in, be denied the benefits of, or be subjected to discrimination under any education program or activity receiving federal financial assistance . . . ."

B. Women Who Did Learn

In the previous essay on women's education, all authors quoted were male. This reflects the fact that it was difficult for a woman to become a writer or even if she did, to have her works known. Nuns, in certain periods at least, were not encouraged to write books, especially ones which would engage them in controversy.[1] Hroswitha, the German nun, did write good Latin plays, but always with the proper moral ending. Some queens, like Margaret of Navarre and Catherine Parr, wrote poems and religious meditations, but they were protected from criticism by their high social position. If a woman had written anything counter to the prevailing views, her works would likely have been ignored or suppressed. The works of the classical Greek woman poet, Sappho, offered an alternative view of women's lives—more erotic than submissive. Her works were burned in early medieval times.[2]

Yet, women participated in the debate over their education largely by their example as educated people. Various time periods witnessed particular groups of learned women. Perhaps there were many more such groups, but if there were, the records have been lost. In early medieval times, Emperor Charlemagne, encouraged women's education in his court; the nuns of Charlemagne's time are thought to have originated the Carolingian script that became the basis of cursive writing.[3] The Anglo-Saxon abbess, Hilda, not only ruled a double monastery of men and

---

[1]Ernest McDonnell, *The Beguines and Beghards in Medieval Culture* (New Brunswick: Rutgers University, 1954), p. 341.

[2]Willis Barnstone, *Sappho* (New York: New York University Press, 1965), p. xxi-xxiii.

[3]Sister Dorothy Irwin, Professor, College of St. Catherine

women, but was known throughout the Christian world for her learning. Other nuns of the medieval era were so well known for their desire to learn that their thoughts were *"compared to a swarm of bees issuing forth from the hive to seek the honey of knowledge."*[4] A manuscript from medieval times shows Hildelith, another Anglo-Saxon abbess, and her nuns eagerly awaiting the bishop's latest book. In 12th century Germany, the abbess Gertrude of Helfta and two of her nuns were noted for their views of a circled universe, which may have influenced the Italian poet, Dante, writing his *Divine Comedy*.[5] Other equally famous educated nuns were Herrade de Landsberg and Hildegard of Bingen.

During medieval times there were educated women who were not religious nuns. Queens such as Eleanor of Aquitaine and other noble women were frequently literate and read religious books. Reading women are frequently pictured in works of art. A favorite subject was the Virgin Mary either reading, being taught to read or surrounded by books.[6] Women not only learned to read but collected books. Medieval marriage customs meant that women were forced to move from their own homes to those of their husbands. Frequently, they carried along books as part of their dowries. Thus, women of the upper classes became cultural ambassadors spreading their native ideas of art, literature and religion to their new homes.[7]

In the period 1350-1600 there was another cluster of exceptionally learned and able women. More and more, learning for women moved from the convent to the court. Now the emphasis was not only on Church learning, but classical learning. It was as important to know

Virgin Mary reading a book

Plato as St. Paul, Seneca as well as Augustine. Learning, at least for upper class women, became fashionable. As one historian of the era put it, *"Not to be classical was to be nothing."*[8] Cardinal Bemo of the Catholic Church said condescendingly, *"Little girls should learn Latin; it completes their charm."*[9]

---

[4]Dorothy Gardiner, *English Girlhood at School* (London: Oxford, 1929), p. 18.

[5]Linda Saport, "Scientific Achievements of Nuns in the Middle Ages," Unpublished Paper, November 25, 1975.

[6]Susan Groag Bell, "Medieval Women Book Owners: Arbiters of Lay Piety and Ambassadors of Culture" *Signs*. Vol. 7, No. 4 (Summer, 1982), p. 761.

[7]*Ibid*. p. 763.

[8]T. Adolphus Trollope, *A Decade of Italian Women* (London: Chapman & Hall, 1859), p. 77.

[9]Myra Reynolds, *The Learned Lady in England* (Boston: Houghton Mifflin, 1920), p. 4.

Christine de Pisan presents a book to a patron.

And little girls did learn Latin—and Greek—and Hebrew. Probably the woman best known for her language ability in the Renaissance was Anna Maria von Schurman (1607-1678) who lived in Utrecht, Holland. She not only knew the ancient languages mentioned but also French, English, Arabic, Chaldee, Syrian and wrote a grammar for Ethopian.[10] The medieval writer Christine de Pisan (1365-c.1431) described herself *"sitting alone in my study, surrounded by books on all kinds of subjects, devoting myself to literary studies, my usual habit . . ."*[11] Sometimes called the first professional woman writer as she received some commissions, she did indeed study hard and produced many great works of literature.

Most of these learned women knew each other by reputation. Some wrote one another, forming a sort of support network to encourage one another's scholarship. Being well educated may have been a status symbol. For example, Lucrezia Borgia was considered to be better looking than her sister-in-law Isabella d'Este, but Isabella used her wit to make Lucrezia feel inferior.[12] But the letters of these educated women, like the exchange between Margaret of Navarre and Vittora Colona, illustrate sympathetic interest. When Catherine of Aragon needed help to prevent her divorce, it was to her former sister-in-law, the intelligent Margaret of Austria, that she wrote for names of lawyers.[13]

The following chart suggests some of the noted women of this era—1400-1600. The criteria for selecting the women for this list has been:

- that they were recognized for their intelligence outside their own country.

- that they understood Latin and perhaps some Greek.

- that they wrote poems or letters that showed at least average ability. Most had at least one book or poem dedicated to them by a male admirer. Many of these women had courts (called salons in France) to which writers came to try out ideas and to display new works.

---

[10]Joyce Irwin, "Anny Maria Van Schurman: The Star of Utrecht," in: J. R. Brink, ed., *Female Scholars: A Tradition of Learned Women before 1800* (Montreal: Eden Press, 1980), p. 70.

[11]Christine de Pizan, *The Book of the City of Ladies,* Earl Jeffrey Richards, tr. (New York: Persea Books, 1982), p. 3.

[12]Julia Cartwright, *Isabella D'Este, Vol. I* (New York: E.P. Dutton, 1911), p. 215-216.

[13]John Paul, *Catherine of Aragon and Her Friends* (London: Burns & Oates, 1966), p. 92.

ENGLAND
Catherine of Aragon
Catherine Parr
Mary Tudor
Lady Jane Grey
Elizabeth I
Mary Sidney
Bathsva Makin
Mildren Cooke Cecil
Anne Cooke Bacon
Margaret Roper
Anne Locke
Jane Fitzalan
Jane Surrey
Elizabeth Russell

SPAIN
Dona Francisca de Nebrija
Dona Lucia de Medrano
Dona Feliciana Enriquez de Guzman
Dona Catalina de Mendoza
Dona Ana Girou
Isabel Clara Eugenia
Luisa Siega
Cecilia Morillas
Oliva de Sabuco
Juana Morella
Isabel de Joya

FRANCE
Margaret of Navarre
Marie de Gournay
Christine de Pisan
Madeline and Catherine des Roches
Madame de Retz
Catherine de Clermont
Marie de Ramieu
Mary Stuart
Margaret de France
Claude, Duchess of
Louise Charly
Louiselabe
Clemence deBourges
Marie de Ramicu Vivaroise
Madeleine Neveau
Catherine de Fradonnet

ITALY
Isabella d'Este
Vittoria Colona
Veronica Gambara
Gaspara Stampa
Ippolita Roma
Giulia Gonzaga
Emila Pia
Tullia D'Aragona
Olympia Morata
Caterina Corner

GERMANY
Margaret VonStaffel
Catherine Von Ostheim
Margaret Welser
Electress Elizabeth
Margaret of Austria
Ann Von Strumm

Are there lasting literary contributions from women on this list? The question is difficult to answer. Women have left no works to compare with the plays of Shakespeare or the poems of Petrarch. Some of their works have been lost and others neglected. Historians are just beginning to look at what is left of women's literary works in light of their significance in social history. For example, Christine de Pisan, a French widow. seems to have been the first European woman who supported herself as a writer. Her books tell us something about how necessary it was for a woman to know how to handle family finances. She also wrote of the need for women to be educated and yet she tried to stay within the pious Christian tradition of her time.

Other than books and poems, the letters of these women comprise a social history of the Renaissance.

The Minneapolis Institute of Arts

Upper class young women, like Jean Clouet portrayed here, were often educated by tutors during the Renaissance.

Many of these women had no time to become polished poets. Some, like Olympia Morata, began brilliantly but were bogged down by marriage and family responsibilities. A letter of hers states: *"My husband [a professor is preparing for his public lectures. I have been excessively busy all day in buying household gear. . ."*[14] It was her husband's career, not her poetry, which took priority. Other literary women, like Isabella d'Este, were equally busy with household duties except that her household was the entire Italian state of Mantua. With her husband away fighting frequent wars, she acted as regent, kept the state together, negotiated treaties and played rather skillfully the rough game of Italian Renaissance politics. Some other women, like Lady Jane Grey of England, were less fortunate. At sixteen, Roger Ascham, a noted scholar recognized her as one of the most promising scholars he had ever met. Lady Jane Grey was caught up in the politics of the era and was made queen—for five days. She was imprisoned in the Tower of London by Queen Mary I and then executed by decapitation. Even though Jane lived only a short time, her letters suggest a strong, intelligent individual.

Belief in women's education comes through clearly, if at times bitterly, in writings of the women of the era from 1500-1600.

"These gentlemen would like to see us [women] plain imbeciles so that we could serve as shadows to set off better their fine wit."
Charlotte de Brachart[15]

"Whoever first forbad them [women] knowledge. . .I believe it is because he had so little learning that he feared they would put him to shame on the second day of their study." Marie de Gournay.[16]

"I cannot but complain of parents in letting the fertile grounds of their daughters lie fallow, and yet send the barren noodles of their sons to the University."
Hannah Woolley[17]

"Is it not foolishly done to hide the talent that God has given us?"
Marie Dentiere[18]

For many of these women, learning was not merely a status symbol but a deeper part of their lives. At times, for both Roman Catholic and Protestant women, it helped to enrich and to console them in their faith. For some, like Elizabeth I, reading history and political theory may have sharpened their administrative ability. For others, learning was a joy in itself. Lady Jane Grey, the unfortunate woman who was briefly a queen, told her tutor how she felt about learning:

"After the usual courtesies had been exchanged Ascham noticed that Lady Jane was reading the Phaedo of Plato, 'with as much delight as if it had been a merry tale of Boccaccio.' 'Why, Madam,' he asked, 'do you relinquish such pastime as going into the park?'

---

[14]Trollope, p. 188.

[15]Ruth Kelso, *Doctrine for the Lady of the Renaissance* (Urbana: University of Illinois, 1956), p. 62-65.

[16]Marjorie Henry Ilsey, *A Daughter of the Renaissance Marie le Jars de Gournay Her Life and Works* (The Hague: Mouton, 1963), p. 57.

[17]Borer, p. 108.

[18]Quoted in Natalie Zenon Davis, *Society and Culture in Early Modern France* (Stanford: Stanford University Press, 1975), p. 82.

She smiled. 'I think all their sport is but a shadow to that pleasure I find in Plato,' she said. As Ascham seemed rather taken aback, she went on, 'Alas! good folk, they never felt what pleasure means.'[19]

Points to Consider

1. What kind of literature was generally seen as proper for women to read and write in medieval times?

2. How did medieval marriage customs make the collecting of books by women an important contribution to the spread of culture?

3. What was Anna Maria von Schurman known for?

4. Why were women chosen to be on the chart?

5. What things do you feel this chart might illustrate?

6. In what ways did these women express their deep desire and longing for learning?

[19]Hester Chapman, *Lady Jane Grey* (Boston: Little Brown, 1962), p. 47,

Chapter 6
Women and the Arts in Medieval/Renaissance Europe

A. Women as Patrons, Poets and Painters

Women appear as the central subjects of many of the great works of medieval and Renaissance literature. For example, there is Beatrice of Dante's "Divine Comedy, Laura of Petrarch's sonnets and the courtly love tradition which placed the Lady on a pedestal for her knight to worship. There are also works like the "Roman de la Rose" by Jean de Meun, which saw women as cynical, grasping, immoral creatures. Female characters in literature often took on the Mary/Eve stereotype. If the female character was good, she was very, very good and likened to the Virgin Mary. If she was bad, she was very, very bad like the Biblical temptress Eve. It took the imagination of a Chaucer or a Shakespeare to see women in more complex ways. Most medieval/Renaissance writers were men who pictured women as either all good or all bad. As Chaucer's character, the wife of Bath said:

*"By god, if women had written stories
As clerks have written their oratories,
They would have written of men more wickedness
Than all the mark of Adam may redress."*

If women themselves had written their own stories, they might have left a more complex picture of their lives and character for 20th century readers to discover.

The Lais of Marie de France in the 12th century, for example, are stories written in poetry, which form some of the "finest medieval short fiction."[1] There are also a few plays,

---

[1] Robert Hanning and Joan Ferrate, *The Lais of Marie de France* (New York: E. P. Dutton, 1978), p. 1.

some brief biographies and some poems by women. But women generally acted as inspirers of great literature. The list of literary men who dedicated books to women is impressive—Boccacio, Erasmus, Castigliano, Rabelais, Chaucer, Petrarch and dozens more. As mentioned earlier, women became important collectors of books and encouraged writers by their patronage. The courts of Italian city-states became centers of literary encouragement by women like Elizabetta and Emile Pia of Urbino or Beatrice d'Este of Milan. A whole cultural phenomenon began with the creation of the salon in France. An intellectual woman opened her home, gathered friends of ability around her who discussed art, politics and philosophy. Women like Margaret of France, Madame and Catherine des Roche, Margaret de Valois and Madame de Rambouillet began this tradition of women holding salons or literary gatherings. This tradition lasts into the 20th century. Their homes were private but offered public space for the exchange of ideas and witticisms apart from the royal courts. Those with ability and good manners knew the way in; dullards, even of wealth and higher class, were less welcome.

However helpful these salons may have been in offering males an audience for their work, they did not necessarily aid women writers. Cultivated women who held salons did offer intellectual role models to younger women and were freer socially to exchange ideas with men than most women. Some of these women, like Madame de Lafayette, author of *Prince de Cleves,* and Madeline de Scudery shared in the French creation of the novel.

By the Renaissance, women poets such as Louise Labe wrote verses that were personal and spoke directly of women's feelings. But earlier, in certain areas of France (particularly in Provence), poets originated the tradition of courtly love in poetry and song. Generally, this tradition was thought of as a male poet offering homage to a female Lady. But there were also women troubadours who sang of love. This 12th century women's poetry still exists although some poems are only fragments. Here, for example, are a few translations of these poems:

Tibors—Thought to have been the earliest woman troubadour.

This is the only part of her poetry still in existence.

"Sweet handsome friend, I can tell you truly that I've never been without desire since it pleased you that I have you as my courtly lover; nor did a time ever arrive, sweet handsome friend,
when I didn't want to see you often: nor did I ever feel regret. Nor did it ever come to pass, if you went off angry, that I felt joy until you had come back: nor..."

Countess of Dia, (Northeast France, 12th century)
Four of her poems have survived.

> *"I've lately been in great distress*
> *over a knight who once was mine,*
> *and I want it known for all eternity*
> *how I loved him to excess.*
> *Now I see I've been betrayed*
> *because I wouldn't sleep with him;*
> *night and day my mind won't rest*
> *to think of the mistake I made.*

> *How I wish just once I could caress*
> *that chevalier with my bare arms*
> *for he would be in ecstasy*
> *if I'd just let him lean his head against my breast.*
> *I'm sure I'm happier with him . . .*
> *My heart and love I offer him,*
> *my mind, my eyes, my life.*

> *Handsome friend, charming and kind,*
> *when shall I have you in my power?*
> *If only I could lie beside you for an hour*
> *and embrace you lovingly—*
> *know this, that I'd give almost anything*
> *to have you in my husband's place,*
> *but only under the condition*
> *that you swear to do my bidding."*[2]

These poems, with their implications of physical love, do not fit the image of the pious, virgin-like medieval/Renaissance woman, nor do the poems of later French poet, Louise Labe. Louise Labe is remarkable because she was the only woman poet of her time in France who was from a simple, lower class family. Some of the women of the family were illiterate. Louise Labe's message to women was **"to lift their minds a little above their distaffs and spindles. . .to apply themselves to science and learning. . ."**[3]

The poems of the women Renaissance troubadours, of Louise Labe and others, do not tell us much about the lives of women in this era, but they do give glimpses of their personal feelings.

[2]Meg Bogin, *The Woman Troubadours* (New York: Paddington Press, 1976), p. 81, 89.

[3]Natalie Zemon Davis, Society and Culture in Early Modern France (Stanford: Stanford University Press, 1975) p. 73-74.

Louise Labe
Renaissance Poet

Kiss me again, again, kiss me again:
I want one of your most delicious ones,
I want one of your most mischievous ones:
I shall give you four, smoldering, in change,

There, do you say it hurts? Let me appease
That wound, ten times tenderly with a kiss,
Thus our lips tangle themselves in bliss;
Let us enjoy each other as we please.

So each one shall lead a double life,
Each his own, each through his lover's life.
But let love add a foolish thought to this:[4]

One writer of prose and poetry did tell more. This was Christine de Pisan who in the late 14th and 15th centuries wrote many important works of literature. In *The Book of the City of Ladies,* she creates a world of historical women with whom she and other allegorical figures carry on discussions. This remarkable book discusses subjects such as the need for complete education for women, the idea that women are often unfairly blamed for inviting rape, the double sexual standard for men and women and violence in marriage. These discussions, as well as the emphasis on women's history and historical contributions are still readable and timely.

Similarly, in the field of medieval/Renaissance art, we have but glimpses of women's abilities and attitudes. The artists of the medieval period were often chose to remain anonymous, making it difficult to distinguish whether works of art were done by male or female artists. We do know that some of the beautiful tapestries and illuminated manuscripts—and some of the more ordinary ones in common—use were signed and done by women who were often nuns. Hildegard of Bingin (1098-1179), Herrad, Abbess of Hohenburg (c. 1190's) and Gisele van Kerssenbrock are just some of the women who acted as illuminators of religious works.[5] Earlier scholars believed that the "Ada School" of calligraphy may have been named after Charlemagne's sister. Even though some scholars now question this, it does suggest that women were active in early manuscript copying.[6] Designers of wall hangings, like Relinde and Harlinde, formed schools where they taught other young women tapestry skills.[7]

---

[4] Quoted In Judith Thurman, "Lost Woman: Louise Labe" *MS* (March, 1980), p. 94.

[5]Germaine Greer, *The Obstacle Race: The Fortunes of Women Painters and Their Work* (New York: Farrar Straus Giroux, 1979), p. 151-168.

[6]*Ibid.*, p. 155.

[7]Karen Petersen, J. J. Wilson, *Women Artists: Recognition and Reappraisal* (New York: Harper & Row, 1976), p. 12-13.

As well as being artists, women were frequently the subjects of medieval art. Women portrayed in medieval art are generally shown in religious piety or at domestic chores. But there are also drawings and statues depicting women musicians, women riding horseback, women offering their books to patrons and even one of a nun and monk on horseback tilting with lances.[8]

During the Renaissance period, individual artists became better known and paintings dealt more frequently with non-religious subjects. Before, convents formed places where women might pursue a career combining art and piety. As convents declined or were enclosed, women artists had to seek patrons and training from secular sources. Marriage and a family often interfered with women's opportunities to join painting schools and to develop patrons who would buy their art. The most common way for a woman to become an artist was to have a father who was one, to learn from him and be able to practice as an artist as part of a family unit.

One of the best women artists of the Renaissance, Artemisia Gentileschi, born in 1593, illustrates this pattern. Her artist-father was Orazio Gentileschi who trained his daughter but not his three sons. A few other women, like Sofonisba Anguissola, came from noble families and received outside professional training.[9] The paintings

of these two women and other Renaissance women artists are now being recognized as maintaining high artistic standards. Among these painters are Lavinia Fontana, Clara Peeters, Giovanna Garzon: Judith Leyster and Louise Moillan.

Religious themes or still lifes are often the subjects of their paintings and do not differ greatly from those chosen by male painters of the era. In many of the paintings however, the women artists stressed strong women. For example, Biblical Judith, who beheaded the tyrant Holofernes, was painted by Artemisia Gentileschi, Elisabetta Sirani and Fede Galizia. The self-portraits by women artists show themselves actively engaged, brushes in hand, like Judith Leyster's "Self-Portrait," or so busy at work that they do not have time to look at the viewer, like Artemisia Gentileschi's "La Pittura."

We have, then, some images of women artists viewing themselves. We also have something of women's lives in the art and literature by women of medieval/Renaissance times. What evidence we have of them is of talented artists' who made lasting contributions to Western civilization.

★ ★ ★ ★ ★ ★

[8]*Ibid.*, p. 11.

[9]Ann Sutherland Harris and Linda Nochlin, *Women Artists: 1550-1950* (New York: Alfred Knopf, 1976), p. 25.

Biblical Judith shown after she beheaded the tyrant, Holofernes.

by Artemisia Gentileschi

"Judith"—Alinari/Art Resource, Inc.

Self-portrait by Artemisia Gentileschi

Points to Consider

1. Why do you think it was more difficult for women than men to become known for their literature?

2. What was the salon tradition?

3. What were some of the themes of women troubadours?

4. How might training for medieval women artists have differed from that of women artists in the Renaissance?

5. How might these women artists have used popular themes in art of their times but made them their own?

6. Compared with men, there are far fewer women artists and writers in medieval/Renaissance times. List as many reasons as you can for there being more men than women writers and artists. Now look over your ideas and choose one answer that seems the best to you and defend your choice in a short paragraph. Select the reason that seems the least good to you and defend your choice in a second short paragraph.

B. Hroswitha of Gandersheim
Nun as Literary Genius

In the l0th century dukedom of Saxony in northern Germany lived a woman who can be viewed as both representative of her place and time and as an exception. Her name was Hroswitha of Gandersheim.

Hroswitha (c. 935-1001) is a representative of 10th century Saxony because:

- By "taking the veil"—becoming a nun[1]—she took advantage of the monastic life encouraged by the dukes of Saxony, especially Otto the Great, who had established monasteries.

- By becoming a writer, she contributed to the high artistic and intellectual character of wealthy, powerful 10th century Saxony.

- By patterning her plays after Latin literature (especially the Roman writer Terence), she followed an older tradition of scholarship that was encouraged by the Saxon dukes' close ties with the Popes in Italy.

However, Hroswitha may be pictured as an exceptional woman because:

- Her six plays "survive as the only evidence of western attempts to write drama in the long period between the fall of the Roman Empire and the invention of the mystery and morality plays of the High Middle Ages."[2]

- She wrote a long poem about Otto the Great's rule as an historical record a hundred years before the histories of Anna Comnena, usually called the first woman historian.[3]

---

[1]Hroswitha was a "canoness" and as such, was allowed somewhat more freedom. She left the convent for outside visits—unlike a regular 10th century nun.

[2]A. Daniel Frankforter, "Sexism and the Search for the Thematic Structure of the Plays of Hroswitha of Gandersheim," *International Journal of Women's Studies,* Vol. 2, No. 3 (May/June, 1979), p. 222.

[3]*Ibid.*, p. 223. Anna (1083-1148) was a Byzantine princess who wrote Byzantine court histories.

- Her works were lost after her death but rediscovered in 1501 by a Renaissance scholar, Conrad Celtes. Celtes was astonished by his discovery and later scholars declared that no woman, especially a nun, would have had the worldly knowledge and high command of Latin to have written these dramas. One 19th century scholar, Joseph von Aschbach, even went so far as to say that the plays were all forgeries. According to Aschbach, Conrad Celtes, aided by friends, forged all of Hroswitha's literary creations as an elaborate joke. Recent scientific tests carried out on the original manuscripts of her plays have proven that they are authentic 10th century works[4] and scholars now accept her as the author.

Little is known of Hroswitha's life except what little she wrote about herself. However, it seems that the most logical explanation of this unusual woman's literary achievements is that her natural genius and scholarly aptitudes were encouraged by the intellectual atmosphere of 10th century Saxony.[5]

Whatever the explanation, her works reveal something more about this woman than mere unique genius. As you read the following excerpt from one of her plays, "Ducitius," note her emphasis upon the battle between Christianity and paganism, the roles or the various women involved in the drama, and the sense or humor that relieves the otherwise serious tone of Hroswitha's story.

---

[4]*Ibid.*, p. 223-224. See also: William Henry Hudson, "Hroswitha of Gandersheim," *English Historical Review,* Vol. 3 (July, 1888), p. 433-434.

[5]10th century Saxony is said to have experienced the "Ottonian Renaissance" named for the intellectual and material achievements found under Otto the Great.

DULCITIUS

SETTING OF THE PLAY: The Roman Empire at the time of the Emperor Diocletian's general persecution of Christians (303 A.D.)

CHARACTERS: The *Roman Governor Dulcitius,* a pagan who actively persecuted local Christians. *Count Sisinnius,* an executioner for Emperor Diocletian. Three "Holy Virgins"—the beautiful Christian maids, *Agape, Chionia and Irena* who are prisoners in their own home and are sought by Dulcitius for evil purposes—probably sexual in nature.

DIALOG FROM THE PLAY

DULCITIUS. "Soldiers, produce your prisoners.
SOLDIERS. The ones you wanted to see are in there.
DULCITIUS. Ye Gods, but these girls are beautiful! What grace, what charm!
SOLDIERS. Perfect!
DULCITIUS. I am enraptured!
SOLDIERS. No wonder!
DULCITIUS. I'm in love! Do you think they will fall in love with me?
SOLDIERS. From what we know, you will have little success.
DULCITIUS. Why?
SOLDIERS. Their faith is too strong.
DULCITIUS. A few sweet words will work wonders!
SOLDIERS. They despise flattery.
DULCITIUS. Then I shall woo in another fashion—with torture!
SOLDIERS: They would not care.
DULCITIUS. What's to be done, then?
SOLDIERS. That is for you to find out.
DULCITIUS. Lock them in the inner room—the one leading out of the passage where the pots and pans are kept.
SOLDIERS. Why there?
DULCITIUS. I can visit them oftener.
SOLDIERS. It shall be done. . .

★ ★ ★ ★ ★ ★

DULCITIUS. What can the prisoners be doing at this hour of night?
SOLDIERS. They pass the time singing hymns.
DULCITIUS. Let us approach.
SOLDIERS. Now you can hear their silver-sweet voices in the distance.
DULCITIUS. Take your torches, and guard the doors. I will go in and enjoy myself in those lovely arms!
SOLDIERS. Enter. We will wait for you here.

★ ★ ★ ★ ★ ★

AGAPE. What noise is that outside the door?
IRENA. It is that wretch Dulcitius.
CHIONIA. Now may God protect us!
AGAPE. Amen.
CHIONIA. There is more noise! It sounds like the clashing of pots and pans and fire-irons.
IRENA. I will go and look. Come quick and peep through the crack of the door!
AGAPE. What is it?

161

IRENA. Oh, look! He must be out of his senses! I believe he thinks that he is kissing us.

AGAPE. What is he doing?

IRENA. No he presses the saucepans tenderly to his breast, now the kettles and frying pans! He is kissing them hard!

CHIONIA. How absurd!

IRENA. His face, his hands, his clothes! They are all as black as soot...

AGAPE. ...His body...is possessed of a devil.

IRENA. Look! He is going now. Let us watch the soldiers and see what they do when he goes out.

★ ★ ★ ★ ★ ★

SOLDIERS. What's this? Either one possessed by the devil, or the devil himself. Let's be off!

DULCITIUS. Soldiers, soldiers! Why do you hurry away? Stay, wait! Light me to my house with your torches.

SOLDIERS. The voice is our master's voice, but the face is a devil's. Come, let's take to our heels! This devil means us no good.

DULCITIUS. I will hasten to the palace. I will tell the whole court how I have been insulted.

★ ★ ★ ★ ★ ★

DULCITIUS. Ushers, admit me at once. I have important business with the Emperor.

USHERS. Who is this fearsome, horrid monster coming here in these filthy rags? Come, let us beat him and throw him down the steps. Stop him from coming further.

DULCITIUS. Ye gods, what has happened to me? Am I not dressed in my best? Am I not clean and fine in my person? And yet everyone who meets me expresses disgust at the sight of me and treats me as if I were some foul monster! I will go to my wife. She will tell me the truth. But here she comes. Her looks are wild, her hair unbound, and all her household follow her weeping.

★ ★ ★ ★ ★ ★

WIFE OF DULCITIUS. My lord, my lord, what evil has come on you? Have you lost your reason, Dulcitius? Have the Christ-worshippers put a spell on you?

DULCITIUS. Now at last I know! Those artful women have made an ass of me!

WIFE OF DULCITIUS. What troubled me most, and made my heart ache, was that you should not know there was anything amiss with you.

DULCITIUS. Those impudent wenches shall be stripped and exposed naked in public. They shall have a taste of the outrage to which I have been subjected!

★ ★ ★ ★ ★ ★

SOLDIERS. [But when soldiers try to disrobe the maids:] Here we are sweating like pigs and what's the use? Their clothes cling to their bodies like their own skin. What's more, our chief, who ordered us to strip them, sits there snoring, and there's no way of waking him. We will go to the Emperor and tell him all that has passed.

★ ★ ★ ★ ★ ★

At last Agape and Chionia are separated from their younger sister, Irena. They face a martyr's death by fire at the hands of the Roman executioner, Count Sisinnius.

CHIONIA. Your Emperor has ordered you to put us to death, and you must obey, as we scorn his decree. If you were to spare us out of pity, you also would die.

162

SISINNIUS. Come, soldiers! Seize these blasphemers and fling them alive into the flames.

SOLDIERS. We will build a pyre at once. The fierceness of the fire will soon put an end to their insolence.

AGAPE. O Lord, we know Thy power! It would not be anything strange or new if the fire forgot its nature and obeyed Thee. But we are weary of this world, and we implore Thee to break the bonds that chain our souls, and to let our bodies be consumed that we may rejoice with Thee in heaven.

SOLDIERS. O wonderful, most wonderful! Their spirits have left their bodies, but there is no sign of any hurt. Neither their hair, nor their garments, much less their bodies, have been touched by the flames!

Finally, Irena also suffers a martyr's death, but only after Count Sisinnius has also been tricked. He was prevented, by a miracle, from carrying out his plan of sending the virgin, Irena, to a brothel:

SISINNIUS. What has happened to me? These Christians have bewitched me. . .

SOLDIERS. . . . If you let this mad-woman live an hour longer it will be the death of us all.

SISINNIUS. Take a bow one of you, bend it as far as you can, and loose a shaft that shall pierce this devilish witch.

SOLDIERS. That's the way!

IRENA. You wretched Sisinnius! Do you not blush for your shameful defeat? Are you not ashamed that you could not overcome the resolution of a little child without resorting to force of arms?

SISINNIUS. I accept the shame gladly, since now I am sure of your death.

IRENA. To me my death means joy, but to you calamity. For your cruelty you will be damned in Tartarus [hell].

But I shall receive the martyr's palm, and, adorned with the crown of virginity, I shall enter the azure palace of the Eternal King, to Whom be glory and honor forever and ever![6]

The Nun, Hroswitha, presenting one of her books to Otto the Great in a print by Albrecht Durer

Points to Consider

1. Did Celtes forge Hroswitha's works? The critic Aschbach believes that he did. Other critics refute this theory, finding it hard to believe.

   Forging six plays, a long historical poem and various other works in 10th century Latin would have been an immense task.

   Even to Aschbach, Celtes seems to have had only weak motivation for forging such documents.

   What reasons might Aschbach have had for developing the elaborate theory that Hroswitha's plays were forged?

   What might his theory say about 19th century attitudes toward women? or about Aschbach's attitude?

2. In the 9th century, after thirty years of warfare, Emperor

Charlemagne forcefully converted Saxony from pagan religions to Christianity. However, it was only in the early 10th century that peoples of Saxony really gave up paganism.

What things in Hroswitha's play indicate that she is concerned with the theme of paganism vs. Christianity?

Why do you think she chose the Roman empire of the time of Diocletian as the setting for the play rather than her own country or, earlier pagan Saxony?

3. What appear to be the outstanding characteristics of:

   Governor Dulcitius

   Agape, Chionia and Irene

   The wife of Governor Dulcitius

   Count Sisinnius

4. How does Hroswitha portray women in this play) What kinds of roles do they play?

5. What personal characteristics does Hroswitha seem to admire most? Why do you think she might find these admirable? Would these characteristics be applicable to both male and female Christian martyrs?

6. Is Dulcitius' wife worried or upset because her husband has tried to sexually abuse three maidens? What is she upset about when she sees Dulcitius and hears what happened to him?

7. Hroswitha must solve a problem in developing her story: Her hero-maids, Agape, Chionia and Irena, are first saved by various miracles but then must die martyr's deaths. How, then, does Hroswitha solve the problem of Agape and Chionia not being saved again by their faith—this time from fiery death?

C. Mary as Mother of the Infant Jesus
An Art Exercise

Medieval times in Europe (c. 800-1450) have frequently been called "the age of faith" because of the great interest of people in religion and because of the power and wealth of the medieval Roman Catholic Church. Medieval art reflects this interest in religion, as nearly all subject matter uses religious themes. The wealth of the Church was used to commission works of art. In France alone, during the 11th century, an estimated 1,587 cathedrals and village churches were built.[1] Each church meant commissions for artists to produce the necessary architectural plans, stained glass windows, decorative wood carvings, sculpture and paintings.

Interest in religious themes, combined with the support of the Church, continued on into the Renaissance (c. 1450-1650). One favorite religious subject throughout both time periods was that of Mary, mother of Jesus, holding the infant Jesus. The following exercise uses just a few of the enormous number of medieval/Renaissance works of art dealing with this theme. The importance to women's history is that Mary became the representation of the ideal woman. The twelve art works selected for this exercise came from different areas of Europe between of 800 and 1500 A.D.

---

[1]Anne Fremantle, *Age of Faith* (New York: Time-Life Books, 1965), p. 122.

Group Task

- Look over these paintings and sculptures of Mary holding the infant Jesus.

- Decide on a person to act as recorder for your group's ideas.

- On three sheets of paper make a list of the dates of each work of art and where they came from in Europe.

LEAVE a space of about ¼ of a page between each. Number the works of art from 1-12.

1. Below each work of art listed, write three specific things that your group uses to describe a specific work of art.

   Now look back over your comments. Write down the adjectives your group used to describe the art, such as beautiful, sweet, lovely or lifelike.

   Note when your group used words like strange, exotic, severe or childlike.

   Write down which paintings or sculptures were the most pleasing to your group. Why? Which were the most interesting. Why?

2. List by number the paintings or sculptures which show Mary looking directly at the viewer.

   Indicate by number the paintings or sculptures where she appears to be looking at the baby.

   List by number when Mary looks away from both the viewer and the baby.

3. In which works of art does Mary wear a crown? Mary was not a ruler or monarch. Of what realm do you think she was considered a queen by these artists?

4. In which works of art does Mary seem to your group to be most like an ordinary woman—one you feel you would recognize if you met her again?

5. One trend of the later Middle Ages—from about c. 1200 to the time of the Renaissance c. 1450—was the growing importance of Mary, mother of Jesus, as a focus of religious prayer. Medieval people increasingly came to pray to her as a divine mother and to view Mary as the ideal, perfect woman. This religious trend of medieval times has been called by historians "the cult of the Virgin Mary." How might this "cult of the Virgin Mary" be seen in the works of art created between 1200 and 1450 shown here? (numbers 6 through 9)

6. It has been said that people of the Renaissance were more interested in this world rather than the next. How might this Renaissance interest in the present life—rather than concentrating on salvation or heaven—be seen in the last three Renaissance paintings shown here? (numbers 10 through 12)

7. What changes do you see in the way artists depict the infant Jesus?

8. Look back over your observations and comments. Write a summary paragraph as a group, describing the historical changes that occurred when artists depicted the mother Mary and infant Jesus in the art of medieval/Renaissance Europe.

9. How might these changes in the way the Virgin Mary was seen have influenced the manner in which ordinary women were treated or viewed by their societies?

From the book of Kells, Ireland, c. 800's A.D.

Carving—The Virgin Mary and Jesus,
Spain, 1000's A.D.

The Golden Madonna
Essen, Germany
900's A.D.

Flight from Egypt, Autun, France, 1130-1135 A.D.

Painting of the Virgin Mary and Jesus
Italy 1200's A.D.

Carving of the
Virgin Mary and Jesus
France 1150-1190 A.D.

Sculpture of the Virgin Mary and Jesus
France 1339 A.D.

Sculpture of the Virgin Mary
and Jesus
France 1300-1500 A.D.

**Painting of the Virgin Mary and Jesus by Lorenzo Monaco
Florence, Italy 1425 A.D.**

"Adoration of the Shepherds"
Painting of The Virgin Mary and Jesus by Domenico
Ghirlandaio
Florence, Italy 1485 A.D.

Virgin Mary and Jesus by Raphael
Italy 1500 A.D.

Madonna of the Rocks by Leonardo da Vinci

Italy 1507 A.D.

Conclusion

The following is a short review and summary of the themes from the book, *Women in Medieval/ Renaissance* using the cultural universals (politics, religion, economics, social arrangements, education and the arts) as an organizing model. Overall, a decline in opportunities for women was seen from medieval times on into the period of the Renaissance.[1] One exception observed is in the area of education for women. By the Renaissance women were permitted a less limited curriculum to study and more women were allowed access to an education.

POLITICS:

Women of the upper classes and royal women in medieval/ Renaissance times frequently held important political positions. The importance of kinship and

inheritance meant that ladies ran manors and estates for absent husbands and controlled land as widows and for minor sons. Royal queens ruled as regents or outright as a regina (queen) for an estimated one fourth of the history of European monarchies. The possibilities for women achieving political power varied, depending on time and place. British women could inherit the throne—as did Mary I and Elizabeth I. French queens could not rule directly as reginas but did so as regents. During the Renaissance,

---

[1]Joan Kelly-Gadol, "Did Women Have A Renaissance?" in *Becoming Visible: Women in European History,* Renate Bridenthal and Claudia Koonz, eds., (Boston: Houghton Mifflin, Co., 1977), p. 148-150.

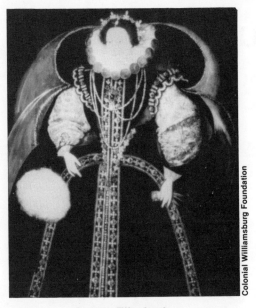

Queen Elizabeth

RELIGION:

In medieval times, there were powerful roles available for religious women within the Roman Catholic Church. Early Christian women served with men in the task of gaining new followers, organizing worship services and giving communion and other sacraments.[5] Beginning in the 4th century, women were excluded from these duties but acted as abbesses of both convents for nuns and of double monastaries which included both men and women communicants. An abbess might have many practical duties but one powerful role of women was that of a mystic, or inspirational leader. Sometimes, as in the case of St. Lioba, a woman could be both spiritual and practical leader of her community of nuns. Medieval religious women were often intellectuals, like Hroswitha and Hildegard who made an impact as writers and philosophers. Others, like Catherine of Siena and Joan of Arc, powerfully influenced political events of their time because of their reputations as exceptionally holy women. During the Renaissance, the Roman Catholic Church suffered a loss of power and prestige. Some reforms within the Church came as a reaction to the Protestant

women, especially in Italy, lost some of their chances for significant political power when compared with medieval times. In the violent political competitions of the Renaissance, fewer powerful positions were inherited with power seized by the force of armies.[2] From the late Middle Ages through the era of the rise of nation states, power became more centralized in much of Europe. The political influence of women generally declined since their political power had usually come from their membership in great feudal land-owning families.[3] Even some military roles for women disappeared as fewer feudal castles needed defending and professional armies were organized by centralized monarchies. Women continued to be quartermasters of these armies—traveling with the soldiers to provide food and clothes as well as clothes washing and nursing services. Women have rarely been given credit in history books for their work.[4] Leadership roles for upper class women tended to disappear in Renaissance European armies.

[2]Joann McNamara and Suzanne F. Wemple, "Sanctity and Power: The Dual Pursuit of Women," in *Becoming Visible: Women in European History*, p. 112.

[3]Barton C. Hacker, "Women and Military Institutions in Early Modern Europe: A Reconnaissance," *Signs*, Volume 6, No. 4 (Summer, 1981), p. 652-653.

[4]See: Suzanne Fonay Wemple, Women in Frankish Society (Philadelphia: University of Pennsylvania Press, 1981).

[5]Ibid., p. 122.

St. Catherine

Reformation in the 16th century, others were begun by earlier critics such as Saint Catherine. One reform was a movement to enclose nuns in convents, with few contacts with the outside world. These religious women were encouraged to maintain a rigorous spiritual life of prayer and contemplation. As contemplatives, these nuns served as religious models for others. What they lost during the enclosure movement was the political influences that religious women such as Saint Catherine of Siena had had in earlier times. Saint Theresa was an important leader in this movement to enclose convents. Saint Theresa gained fame and a reputation for special holiness by way of her religious writings—but also because she left her walled convent to travel throughout Spain founding new convents.

Although nuns and religious women continued to have influence within the Roman Catholic Church, the roles for religious women, during Renaissance times, were restricted when compared with the wider choices available in medieval times. More women than men broke away from Catholicism at various times to join groups like the Waldenses who were declared heretical by the Roman Catholic Church in 1215. Women who joined religious sects were often persecuted and sometimes suffered torture and death for their beliefs. During the Protest Reformation, women formed a major part of those that left the Church to join the dissenters. Perhaps the fact that they were excluded from the ruling Church hierarchy of priest to Pope and that their options were restricted when compared with earlier times, made them more eager to join new religious communities. Whether these women dissenters improved their situation by leaving the Roman Catholic Church and what new roles and opportunities were opened to them in the Protestant Reformation are still being debated by historians.

ECONOMICS:

Women during medieval times were active in numerous occupations depending on their time, class and circumstance. Peasant women worked hard at farm labor of all kinds—planting, tending and harvesting crops, preserving food, caring for animals and doing domestic tasks. Ladies of medieval manors acted as supervisors of the many crucial tasks of the home economies. Their control over the manors depended on such factors as the area in which they lived or whether they were single, married or widowed. Under Roman law women had equal rights of inheritance with men. Under Germanic laws, women did not inherit from their own family as did their brothers but gained access to land control only through marriage. Women in medieval/ Renaissance times did work at numerous occupations. They were weavers, sewers of clothes, beer makers, tavern keepers, money

The plagues of the Black Death in the 14th century seem to have killed more men than women. Even though women faced the perils of childbirth, frequent wars again caused a sex imbalance that at times favored women. Therefore, women's historians are now reconsidering these eras with the idea that more single, *femme soles* controlled property and ran estates. Also, this sex imbalance may have contributed to the accusations made against women as witches. Older women may have been especially vulnerable to attack because they were often left alone in situations of poverty in medieval/Renaissance villages.[6]

lenders, sellers of merchandise, midwives, medics and teachers, to mention just a few common occupations. Some women were wealthy and gave money to create new convents or other charity projects. Many women were very poor and worked at strenuous physical tasks such as farm work or heavy domestic chores. Some got no pay at all, only room and board.

Family historians are also calling into question a picture of a close relationship of parents to children in earlier times. There seems little evidence to support the idea that extended families living together were common. Perhaps the strongest proof of weak family ties was the practice of infanticide, especially female infanticide, prevalent in medieval Europe.[7]

killing of an infant

SOCIAL ARRANGEMENTS:

Recent history concerning the family questions conventional ideas of women's marital status and family roles in medieval/Renaissance times. Population or demographic studies using data and computers indicate that far more women lived as single people than was previously thought. The number of widows was high. Nuns, of course, were unmarried. Long absences of men on Crusades or off to war meant that women frequently were alone—and in charge—at home. It has also been found that at various times and places there were rather large groups of older, always single women.

[6]See: Alan Macfarlane, The Origins of English Individualism: The Family, Property and Social Transition (New York: Cambridge University Press, 1978) and Jeffrey Russell, Witchcraft in the Middle Ages (Ithaca: Cornell University Press, 1972) and H.C. Erik Midelfort, Witchhunting in Southwestern Germany (Stanford: Stanford University Press, 1972).

[7]Emily Coleman, "Infanticide in the Early Middle Ages," in Women in Medieval Society, Susan Mosher Strand, ed., (Philadelphia: University of Pennsylvania Press, 1976), p. 47-70.

Swimming a witch

Other issues for women within the social setting of medieval/ Renaissance Europe might be summarized by the idea of the dual view of women: Mary vs. Eve; saint vs. witch; the pedestal vs. the stake. Achieving the ideal of the Virgin Mary as mother was not possible for normal women and the depravity of the witch did not represent reality. The social insistence in medieval/Renaissance of viewing women in a dualistic, unrealistic way caused serious social problems. It was especially mischievious when used as a reason for accusing some women of practicing witchcraft. As historian E. William Monter commented about medieval/ Renaissance history, *"the sad truth is that, in women's 'real' social history, the pedestal is almost impossible to find, but the stake is everywhere."*[8]

EDUCATION FOR WOMEN:

During the Renaissance, the idea that women could be educated gained ground. With the rise of a humanist philosophy which advocated a classical education for women, some women, at least those of the upper classes—were educated. The curriculum for these women's educations went beyond the traditional subjects which had been limited to religious or domestic subjects. Therefore, the major gain for women in the Renaissance might be seen in the area of education.

Even in medieval times there were important exceptional women who attained a high degree of learning. Nuns like Hroswitha and Hildegard achieved intellectual excellence in a number of areas. Renaissance women who had not followed a religious vocation had new opportunities for scholarly study, and the argument over whether women could learn found fewer defenders than in medieval times.

Christine de Pisan

---

[8]E. William Monter, "The Pedestal and the Stake: Courtly Love and Witchcraft," in Becoming Visible, p. 135.

WOMEN AND THE ARTS:

Women were artists and writers throughout this long period of medieval/Renaissance times. During medieval times there are indications that nuns were frequently craftspeople creating tapestries, manuscripts and carvings. There was a large demand for crafts for the enormous number of churches and also for decorating manor houses and castles. Much of this artistic work was done anonymously. Decorations for cathedrals and churches were done for the glory of God, not to bring personal credit to the artist. Because artistic works were often not signed, it is difficult to know whether women or men did the carving and decorative works on medieval cathedrals. It is known that there were women artists.

Art of the Renaissance was usually produced by artists who were neither nuns nor monks. The Church continued to be the major patron of the artists and artists still favored religious subjects. They signed their works and were interested in receiving credit for their artistic creations. There were fewer women than men who became artists because most women did not receive the necessary training. Some did, however, receive lessons from relatives—especially daughters from their artist-fathers. A few achieved greatness. Other women created works of art in tapestry and other types of handwork that were more usual for women. These craftswomen could more readily receive training from other women as a part of their education. While young men wishing to be painters or sculptors might be apprenticed to an artist (usually male) this was not considered proper for young women.

Women in the medieval/Renaissance times participated and contributed in all areas of human life. If their story has not been told as frequently as that of men, perhaps it is because they were not always as visible. Still, women as queens, military defenders, writers, artists, saints, accused witches, philosophers and in countless other roles made their impact on this long period of history.

Self portrait by Artemisia Gentileschi

SELECTED BIBLIOGRAPHY: WOMEN IN MEDIEVAL/RENAISSANCE EUROPE

* Starred items are particularly valuable sources for students.

Biography

* Bainton, Roland. *Women of the Reformation in France and England.* Boston: Beacon Press, 1973.

* ____ . *Women of the Reformation in Germany and Italy.* Boston: Beacon Press, 1971.

* ____. *Women of the Reformation from Spain to Scandinavia.* Minneapolis: Augsburg Press, 1977.

Calder-Marshall, Arthur. *The Two Duchesses.* New York: Harper & Row, 1978.

Chapman, Hester. *Lady Jane Grey.* Boston: Little Brown, 1962.

_____ . *Mary II: Queen of England.* Westport, CT: Greenwood, 1976, (1953).

_____ . *Two Tudor Portraits: Henry Howard and Lady Katherine Gray.* London: Jonathan Cape, 1960.

Dahmus, Joseph. *Seven Medieval Queens.* Garden City: Doubleday, 1972.

Durant, David. *Bess of Hardwick: Portrait of an Elizabethan Cynast, 1527-1608.* London: Weidenfeld and Nicolson, 1977.

Einhard. *The Life of Charlemagne.* Evelyn Firchow and Edwin Zeyclel, Tra. Coral Gables, FL: University of Miami Press, 1972.

Erlanger, Philippe. *Margaret of Anjou: Queen of England.* London: Elek Books, 1970.

* Erlanger, Rachel. *Lucrezia Borgia.* New York: Hawthorn/Dutton, 1978.

Fink, Greta. *Great Jewish Women.* New York: Menorah Publishing, 1978.

* Gies, Frances and Joseph, *Women in the Middle Ages.* New York: Thomas Crowell, 1978.

Haight, Anne Lyon, ed. *Hroswitha of Gandersheim.* New York: Hroswitha Club, 1965.

Haslip, Joan. *Lucrezia Borgia.* Indianapolis: Bobbs/Merrill, 1953.

Haswell, Jock. *The Ardent Queen: Margaret of Anjou and the Lancastrian Heritage 1429-1482.* London: Peter Davies, 1976.

Hogrefe, Pearl. *Tudor Women: Commoners and Queens.* Ames: Iowa State, 1975.

_____ . *Women of Action in Tudor England.* Ames: Iowa State, 1977.

Jenkins, Elizabeth. *Elizabeth the Great.* New York: Coward/McCann, 1958.

* Kelly, Amy. *Eleanor of Aquitaine and the Four Kings.* London: Harvard University Press, 1950.

Kibler, William. *Eleanor of Aquitaine: Patron and Politician.* Austin: University of Texas Press, 1976.

Levine, Joseph. *Elizabeth I.* Englewood Cliffs: Prentice Hall, 1969.

* Lofts, Norah. *Anne Boleyn.* New York: Coward, McCann & Geoghagen, 1979.

* _____. *Queens of Britain.* London: Hodder and Stoughton, 1977.

* Lowenthal, Marvin, tr. *The Memoirs of Gluckel of Hameln.* New York: Schocken Books, 1977.

Lucie-Smith, Edward. *Joan of Arc.* New York: W.W. Norton, 1976.

Marek, George. *The Bed and the Throne: The Life of Isabella d'Este.* New York: Harper and Row, 1976.

Marshall, Rosalind. *The Days of Duchess Anne: Life in the Household of the Duchess of Hamilton 1656-1716.* New York: St. Martin's Press. 1973.

Martiensson, Anthony. *Queen Katherine Parr.* New York: McGraw Hill, 1973.

Mattingly, Garrett. *Catherine of Aragon.* London: Jonathan Cape, 1950.

Maurois, Andre. *Adrienne: The Life of the Marquise de la Fayette.* New York: McGraw Hill, 1961.

Mayer, Dorothy Moulton. *The Great Regent: Louise of Savoy, 1476-1531.* London: Weidenfeld and Nicolson, 1966.

McLeod, Enid. *The Order of the Rose.* New Jersey: Rowman and Littlefield, 1976.

* Meade, Marion. *Eleanor of Aquitaine.* New York: Hawthorn Books, 1977.

Mitford, Nancy. *Madame de Pompadour.* London: Hamish Hamilton, 1954.

Mossiker, Frances. *The Affair of the Poisons.* New York: Alfred Knopf, 1969.

Paul, John. *Catherine of Aragon and Her Friends.* London: Burns & Oates, 1966.

* Power, Eileen. *Medieval People.* New York: Barnes & Noble, 1963.

* Roelker, Nancy. *Queen of Navarre: Jeanne d'Albret.* Cambridge: Belknap press, 1968.

Sackville-West, V. *Daughter of France: The Life of Anne Marie Louise d'Orleans Duchesse de Montpensier.* London: Michael Joseph, 1959.

_____. *Saint Joan of Arc.* London: Michael Joseph, 1936.

Seward, Desmond. *Eleanor of Aquitaine.* New York: Times Books, 1979.

Undset, Sigrid. *Catherine of Siena.* Kate Austine-Lund, tr. London/New York: Sheed and Ward, 1954.

Wainwright, F.T. "Aethelflaed Lady of the Mercians" in *The Anglo-Saxons,* Peter Clemoes, ed. London: Bowes & Bowes, 1959.

Williams, Neville. *Elizabeth the First: Queen of England.* New York: E.P. Dutton, 1968.

Non-Fiction

Adam, Isabel. *Witch Hunt, The Great Scottish Witchcraft Trials of 1697.* London: Macmillan, 1978.

Alberti, Leon Battista. *The Family in Renaissance Florence.* Columbia, SC: University of South Caroline Press, 1969.

* Baker, Derek, ed. *Medieval Women.* Oxford: Basil Blackwell, 1978.

Baroja, Julio Caro. *The World of the Witches.* Chicago: University of Chicago, 1964.

Bingham, Stella. *Ministering Angels.* Oradell, NJ: Medical Economics Company, Book Division, 1979.

* Bogin, Meg. *The Women Troubadours.* New York: Paddington Press, 1976.

Borer, Mary Cathcart. *Willingly to School: A History of Women's Education.* London: Lutterworth, 1976.

Brink, J.R. *Female Scholars: A Tradition of Learned Women Before 1800.* Montreal: Eden Press, 1980.

Clark, Elizabeth and Herbert Richardson, eds. *Women and Religion: A Feminist Sourcebook of Christian Thought.* New York: Harper & Row, 1977.

* Donnison, Jean. *Midwives and Medical Men.* New York: Schocken Books, 1977.

Eckenstein, Lina. *Woman Under Monasticism.* Cambridge: Cambridge Press, 1896.

Greer, Germaine. *The Obstacle Race.* New York: Farrar Straus Giroux, 1979.

Haining, Peter, ed. *The Witchcraft Papers.* London: Robert Hale & Company, 1974.

* Harksen, Sibylle. *Women in the Middle Ages.* New York: Abner Schram, 1975.

* Henry, Sondra and Emily Taitz. *Written Out of History.* New York: Bloch Pub., 1978.

* Kelly-Gadol, Joan. "Did Women Have a Renaissance?" in *Becoming Visible: Women in European History.* Renate Bridenthal and Claudia Koonz, eds. Boston: Houghton Mifflin, 1977.

* Kelso, Ruth. *Doctrine for the Lady of the Renaissance.* Urbana: University of Illinois Press, 1956.

Kieckhefer, Richard. *European Witch Trials: Their Foundations in Popular and Learned Culture 1300-1500.* Berkeley & Los Angeles: University of California Press, 1976.

* Koltun, Elizabeth, ed. *The Jewish Woman.* New York: Schocken Books, 1977.

* Kors, Alan and Edward Peters, eds. *Witchcraft in Europe.* Philadelphia: University of Pennsylvania Press, 1972.

McLaughlin, Eleanor. "The Christian Past: Does it Hold a Future for Women," in *Womenspirit Rising.* Carol P. Christ and Judith Plaskow, eds. San Francisco: Harper & Row, 1979.

Maclean, Ian. *The Renaissance Notion of Woman.* Cambridge: Cambridge University Press, 1980.

_____. *Woman Triumphant: Feminism in French Literature 1610-1652.* Oxford: Calrendon Press. 1977.

* McNamara, JoAnn and Suzanne Wemple. "Sanctity and Power: The Dual Pursuit of Medieval Women," in *Becoming Visible: Women in European History.* Renate Bridenthal and Claudia Koonz, eds. Boston: Houghton Mifflin, 1977.

Marwick, Max, ed. *Witchcraft and Sorcery.* Middlesex, England: Penguin Books, 1970.

Midelfort, H.C. Erik. *Witch Hunting in Southwestern Germany 1562-1684.* Stanford CA: Stanford University Press, 1972.

* Monter, E. William. *European Witchcraft.* New York: John Wiley & Sons, Inc., 1969.

Morewedge, Rosemarie, ed. *The Role of Women in the Middle Ages.* Albany: State University of New York Press, 1975.

* Morris, Joan. *The Lady Was a Bishop.* New York: Macmillan, 1973.

* Pagels, Elaine. *The Gnostic Gospels.* New York: Random House, 1979.

Peel, Edgar and Pat Southern. *The Trials of the Lancashire Witches.* New York: Taplinger Publishing Co., 1969.

Power, Eileen. *Medieval English Nunneries c. 1275-1535.* Cambridge: Cambridge University Press, 1922.

Priesand, Rabbi Sally. *Judaism and the New Woman.* New York: Behrman House, 1975.

Rosen, Barbara, ed. *Witchcraft.* London: Edward Arnold, 1969.

Ruether, Rosemary, ed. *Religion and Sexism.* New York: Simon and Schuster, 1974.

Russell, Jeffrey B. *Witchcraft in the Middle Ages.* Ithaca, NY: Cornell University Press, 1972.

Sebald, Hans. *Witchcraft: The Heritage of a Heresy.* New York: Elsevier, 1978.

Seth, Ronald. *Stories of Great Witch Trials.* London: Arthur Barker Ltd., 1967.

Stenton, Doris. *The English Woman in History.* New York: Schocken Books, 1977.

Stone, Lawrence. *The Family, Sex and Marriage: In England 1500-1800.*
New York: Harper & Row, 1977.

* Stuard, Susan Mosher. *Women in Medieval Society.* Philadelphia:
University of Pennsylvania Press, 1976.

Swidler, Leonard. *Biblical Affirmations of Woman.* Philadelphia:
Westminster Press, 1979.

_____. *Women in Judaism: The Status of Women Formative Judaism.*
Metuchen, NJ: The Scarecrow Press, 1976.

Warner, Marina. *Alone of All Her Sex: The Myth and the Cult of the
Virgin Mary.* New York: Alfred Knopf, 1976.

Wemple, Suzanne. *Women in Frankish Society: Marriage and the
Cloister 500-900.* Philadelphia: University of Pennsylvania Press, 1981.

Glossary

Anglo-Saxon Era: The period of English history after the fall of the Roman Empire and beginning with the Christian Era until the Norman conquest of England by William the Conqueror in 1066 A.D.

Abbess: A woman who is the superior or leader of a convent of nuns (usually of the Roman Catholic faith). In medieval times there were abbesses who were also heads of double monasteries which had both nuns and monks.

Academic Medicine: In medieval/Renaissance times it meant doctors or other practitioners trained at universities rather than those who learned medicine mostly from experience.

Apprentice: A person who is legally bound to serve another person for a specified length of time with the idea of learning a trade or skill. In medieval times children were frequently apprenticed at an early age.

Archaeology/ Archaeological: The study of the ancient past, particularly through artifacts and other non-written remains.

Ascetic: A person who practices extreme self-denial and self-discipline, one who frequently spends time in religious contemplation — going without food, sleep and bodily comforts.

Ballads: Term often used as a song with a narrative or story.

Barbarians: In late Roman and early medieval times they were the non-Christian non-literate groups of tribal peoples from Northern Europe who invaded Rome. The term "barbarian" as applied to these groups has been questioned by some modern historians.

Bequests: Goods or money handed down through a will.

Beguines: Groups of medieval women who lived religious lives, were interested in doing charity, but were not bound by religious vows such as nuns often living individually though near one another.

Black Death: Also called the black plague or the bubonic plague. This epidemic disease killed one third of all Europeans in the mid-14th century. It continued to reoccur in Europe through the 18th century.

Broadsides: Advertisements or announcements printed cheaply and quickly on one side of a sheet of paper — meant for wide distribution.

Bulls: An edict or pronouncement by the Pope as the leader of the Roman Catholic Church.

Burgundian: A person from the area of France (Gaul) called Burgundy.

Caesarean Section:	To remove an infant from the womb by surgically cutting open the mother and taking the baby. The operation is named after Julius Caesar who was born in such a manner.
Canonize:	To declare a person, after death, a saint of the Roman Catholic Church.
Cardinal:	Men appointed by the Pope — head of the Roman Catholic Church — to make up his council or college of cardinals. Cardinals are next in power to the Pope in the hierarchy of the church.
Capetian:	Relating to the French royal house or family founded in the 10th century that ruled France in direct line until 1328.
Carolingian:	Early medieval family that was of Frankish origin and ruled France from the 8th to 10th centuries. Most famous of these rulers was Charlemagne who temporarily united Europe in the 9th century. (See also: Merovingian).
Celts/Celtic:	One of the Pre-Roman, Iron Age peoples of Europe especially associated with parts of the British Isles such as Ireland, Scotland, and Wales.
Chaldee:	Ancient middle Eastern language of the Semitic Chaldean peoples who lived in the area of South Babylonia in Biblical times.
Charisma:	Can mean a spiritual gift to be able to heal but has come to mean a mystical ability to lead people.
Chastity:	Abstention from sexual intercourse.
Chivalry:	Gallant behavior or the code of honor practiced by medieval knights which meant their being especially kind to ladies.
Chronicles:	An historical account usually put in order of events and in time sequence but without discussion — frequently, as used here, an ancient historic account.
Concubine:	In medieval times, this term usually meant a woman who was living continously with a man over a long period of time but was considered to have contracted an inferior, non-official marriage which was not authorized by the Church.
Consecrate:	To induct a person into an office with a religious rite or ceremony.
Counter-Reformation:	The response of the Roman Catholic Church to the Protestant Reformation of the 16th century. It combined reform within the Catholic Church with an effort to win back church members.

Courtly Love: A tradition in late medieval times (12th to 14th centuries) which stresses romantic rules of conduct between lovers, not necessarily husband and wife.

Consort: The married partner of a queen or king who may have had a lot of power, or a little, depending on factors such as custom, law, or personality.

Convent: Means assembly or community of monks or nuns — a group of religious men/women who usually live separately from society so as to maintain a particularly religious life.

Crusades/ Crusading: From the late 11th century to the 13th century Europeans conducted at least seven expeditions to Palestine, to recover the "Holy City" of Jerusalem from the Muslims, considered to be infidels or non-believers by Christian Europeans.

Cult of the Virgin: The medieval movement that raised Mary, mother of Jesus, to an extremely high position — one where she was almost worshipped.

Cursive Writing: Flowing or writing formed with connecting strokes (in contrast to printing — including ancient Latin script). The system perfected in the 8th century was called the "Carolingian minuscule" that became the predecessor for modern western handwriting.

Dauphin: The title of the Crown Prince or future king of France.

Demography: Study of population — especially using statistical anaylsis of the growth and the distribution of peoples.

Dissenters: People who disagree with the established Church.

Domestic Workers: Servants who work for others in their employer's homes or estates as maids, cooks, gardeners, etc.

"Double" Monastaries: An abbess or abbot in medieval times might lead a convent of nuns/monks who lived as part of one religious institution — but not in the same area.

Dowager: A widow who has usually inherited some property from her late husband — and kept her title acquired from him — such as the "Empress Dowager" or "Duchess Dowager."

Dower: Real estate given by law to the widow from her dead husband — at least for her use during her lifetime.

Empirics: Those medical people who learned medicine by experience and from other practitioners.

Enclosed/ Enclosure: (of convents) To keep the nuns from contact with wordly outside influence, there was a movement from the 15th century on to make the convents separate from their communities and have nuns keep strict religious "rule."

Excommunicate: To be officially shut out of the church and be refused the rites of the church like communion or extreme unction at death.

Fertility: As used here, means human pregnancy and birth — reproduction of children.

Franks: A confederacy of Germanic tribes of Western Europe.

Ghettos: The quarter or area of European medieval/Renaissance towns and cities where Jews were required to live.

Gnostic: A follower of a philosophical and religious movement of early Christianity. Gnostic ideas were later declared heretical by the Roman Catholic Church.

Governess: A woman who teaches a child or children — especially a woman hired by a family to teach or tutor their children.

Guild: In medieval times, associations of merchants or people in trades/crafts formed to protect the business interests of their members. Frequently they acquired political power as well.

Heresy/Heretic: Religious beliefs held by individuals or groups contrary to the authorized doctrines of any particular church. In medieval times the church authority in Western Europe was that of the Roman Catholic Church. A heretic is one accused of heresy or one who holds unauthorized beliefs.

Hierarchy: A system where persons are ranked one above the other as in the Roman Catholic Church where the bottom rank was parish priest, then bishop, archbishop, cardinal and, finally the pope at the top.

Holy Land: For Christians, the Holy Land is Palestine where Jesus lived and conducted his ministry — especially holy would be the city of Jerusalem.

Huguenots: French Protestants of the 16th and 17th centuries — usually followers of John Calvin's religious beliefs.

Humors: In ancient/medieval medicine one of four bodily fluids (blood, phlegm, yellow bile and black bile) that were thought to regulate a person's health and also their temperament.

Infanticide: **(in-FAN-ticide)** The killing of babies usually soon after birth for various reasons — poverty, population problems, or because the sex of the baby made it unwanted.

Infidels: Non-Christian or unfaithful to Christianity; Muslims were called by this term in medieval times.

Judaism/Jews:	A major world religion, Jews (followers of Judaism) hold to the ideas of the Bible but not those of the New Testament. From Roman times, Jews made up the largest non-Christian minority group in Europe.
Jurisdiction:	Authority or legal power to govern, control or pass laws.
The Lady:	In medieval times was the title referring to the woman admired by a troubadour or knight — an aspect of the ideas of Courtly Love. It also is the proper title for a woman whose husband is a higher rank than a knight.
Latin:	Language used by the Ancient Romans. Latin was the ceremonial language of the Roman Catholic Church until recently.
Mancuses:	An Anglo-Saxon measurement of gold or silver equal to 30 pence (or pennies).
Mania:	To do with madness — a passionate or unreasonable belief.
Martyr:	A person, who by refusing to renounce his religious beliefs, voluntarily suffers torture and death.
Matron:	A wife or widow but it usually refers to a woman who has borne children.
Medieval:	The Middle Ages or roughly that time period in European history from the fall of the Roman Empire (476 A.D.) to the 15th century.
Medievalists:	Those scholars that study and are interested in medieval times.
Merovingian:	Refers to the first Frankish royal family or dynasty in France (Gaul) founded in 481 A.D. by Clovis I. In 751 Pepin the Short disposed the Merovingian king and became the first of the Carolingians to rule.
Middle Ages:	Means the same time period as *medieval* European history, c. 476 to the 15th century.
Midwife/ Midwifery: (mid-WI-fery)	One who assists at the birth of babies or the practice of assisting at childbirths. In medieval times frequently was an experienced woman from a village with no formal training or one who learned from another midwife. (See also: empiric).
Misogynist/ Misogyny:	A person who hates or dislikes women or the characteristic of being anti-woman as in misogynistic literature.
Missionaries:	In early medieval times, those who preached Christianity to pagans (non-Christians).

Monasteries:	A place where monks or nuns went to live a spiritual life under religious vows. In modern times, this term usually means a religious retreat for monks while the term convent is used for nuns.
Monks:	Males under religious vows who try to live spiritual existences in monasteries.
Moors:	Muslims from North Africa, (the term comes from the name of Morocco), who conquered and occupied Spain until 1492.
Mosaics:	Pictures created from tiny colored stones cemented in plaster. Often large wall murals or floor designs.
Muslims:	A follower of the religion Islam which was founded by the Prophet Muhammad, in Arabia in 622 A.D.
Mystical/Mystic:	Having spiritual experiences or direct communication to God through contemplation or visions. One who has these experiences is a mystic.
Nun/Nunnery:	A woman who takes religious vows to try to live a particularly holy or spiritual life. A nunnery is a place where nuns live, often separated from the secular world. (see also convent, secular).
Orthodox:	The approved or correct doctrine or belief.
Pagan/Paganism:	In medieval times, one who was not a Christian, they included people who believed in many gods in nature or in ancestor worship. Paganism is the term used by Christians to describe such beliefs.
Patron:	In medieval/Renaissance terms, an individual person or institution (especially the Roman Catholic Church) which supported an artist or writer while she/he produced a work of art.
Pilgrimage:	A journey taken to an especially holy place seeking favors from God (for example a woman might pray for a child) or to gain forgiveness for a sin.
Pious:	A person whose focus is especially spiritual and focuses on religious concerns rather than worldly pleasures.
Polyandry:	The practice of having more than one husband at one time.
Polygamy/Polygamous:	The practice of having more than one spouse at the same time.
Polygyny:	The practice of having more than one wife at one time.
The Pope:	The head of the Roman Catholic faith whose headquarters is usually at the Vatican, in Rome, Italy.
Pragmaticism:	Pertaining to the practical, the value of actions are tested by the earlier conditions and its results.

Precepts:	Orders or commands meant as rules of conduct — practical rules to guide an individual's behavior.
Protestant Reformation:	From to protest, this is a term used to describe a number of reform movements begun by such people as Martin Luther and John Calvin to change the Roman Catholic Church. The result was a number of separate faiths outside of Roman Catholicism.
Recant:	To take back or retract (especially public) opinions or beliefs.
Recluse:	A person who lives completely alone in seclusion, sometimes as a hermit.
Reformation:	From to reform or to change for the better (see Protestant Reformation).
Regent/Regency:	One who rules for another; in medieval/Renaissance times this frequently meant a Dowager Queen ruling for her minor oldest son until he gained his majority or official adulthood and became the ruling king. Regency — the office of regent.
Renaissance:	Literally new birth — this was an important era of European history from the 15th to mid-17th century in which people became impressed with both ideas that would lead to modern science and a renewed interest in the classical past of ancient Greece and Rome.
Roman Catholic Church:	The dominant and only widely accepted uniting religious power in Western Europe in medieval times. A Christian faith characterized by a hierarchy (priest to Pope — See: hierarchy), strictly defined doctrine and massive following of Europeans — many converted from pagan beliefs.
Roman Empire:	From the time of Julius Caesar (d. 44 B.C.) to the fall of Rome to tribal people (476 A.D.). This was the great political power that regulated much of the Middle East and Europe politically and economically.
Salic Law.	A rule of succession in some noble or royal families in Europe which did not permit women (or those descended from the females' line) to succeed to titles or offices — such as queen. The basis was a mistaken idea that it was a law of the Salian Franks. (See: Franks).
Salon:	A European institution in which women of wit, intelligence and social standing encouraged artists, writers, philosophers and political thinkers by providing a meeting place in their homes. In these women's homes, intellectuals could meet to discuss ideas and share in their artistic accomplishments.

Scapegoats:	A person or group of people bearing the blame for events or for the actions of others for which they are not at fault.
Secular:	Things of this world in contrast to spiritual or eternal concerns.
Siege:	An army surrounding and waiting out the surrender of a city, town, or castle in medieval times.
Spanish Inquisition:	Established by Queen Isabella and King Ferdinand in 1478 (it was not directly connected to the medieval Inquisition of the Catholic Church that sought out heretics). It became a kind of secret police in service mostly to Spanish monarchs — it was abolished in Spain in 1820.
Status:	The position an individual has in society — in medieval times one's status would usually be closely connected to one's class, with peasant being a low class and noble or royalty, upper class.
Stereotypes:	Attributing an individual's characteristics (physical, mental or temperamental) to a whole class, sex, religious group or nationality.
Synagogue/ Temple:	Synagogue is literally a meeting together or gathering of Jews for public worship. The synagogue was a building to meet and worship in, a temple for Jews went back to the three successively destroyed temples in Jerusalem.
Talmud:	Sixty-three books of commentaries by scholars who, over 1,000 years, interpreted the first five books of the Bible or Torah — next to the Torah, the Talmud is the basis of Jewish faith.
Theology/ Theologian:	To do with knowledge of God and religion — the study of religious beliefs. A theologian is one who studies, writes, or teaches religion (often a member of the clergy).
Torah:	First five books of the Bible or *The Five Books of Moses*. The study of Torah was considered a required activity for medieval Jewish men.
Virgin Mother:	Refers to the mother of Jesus, Mary, considered by Roman Catholic doctrine to be a Virgin when she conceived Jesus, thus she was the Virgin Mother.
Visionary:	An individual known for great imagination whose ideas may not seem to have had an immediate practical application but occasionally these ideas are far ahead of their time.
Ward/Wardship:	Person under the legal control of another; (literally under guard, thus under control of a guardian). Wardship, then, is the state of being under a guardian.

Wet Nurse: A woman who has borne a child and, thus, is lactating (has milk). She may suckle a child not her own for pay. A common medieval/Renaissance custom was to send babies to be nursed in this way rather than by their actual mother.

Wise Women: A village women — often elderly — known for her knowledge of herbs, healing and perhaps some low magic such as foretelling events, love charms, etc.

Zeal/Zealot: Having a passionate interest usually religious. A person with fanatically passionate enthusiasm for a cause.

ABOUT THE AUTHORS

Susan Hill Gross was born in Minnesota and received her B.A. Degree from the University of Minnesota and her M.A. Degree in History from the College of William and Mary. Ms. Gross taught secondary English and history in Denbigh, Virginia, Savannah, Georgia and the Robbinsdale Schools in Minnesota before becoming a director of the curriculum project Women in World Area Studies. She served on the Robbinsdale Central Committee for student affairs, as treasurer of the Minnesota Council for the Social Studies and is presently recorder for WHOM (Women Historians of the Midwest). She is currently co-director of the Upper Midwest Women's History Center for Teachers.

Marjorie Wall Bingham was born in St. Paul, Nebraska, received a B.A. Degree from Grinnell College and M.A. and Ph.D. degrees from the University of Minnesota. She has taught high school history for the St. Louis Park school system since 1963. Dr. Bingham's experience also includes teaching in a junior high school in Davenport, Iowa and at the University of Minnesota. She is presently co-director of WWAS (Women in World Area Studies), a member of the Minnesota Council for the Social Studies Executive Board, past member of the Education Board of the Minnesota Historical Society and past President of WHOM (Women Historians of the Midwest).

Ms. Gross and Dr. Bingham have been invited frequently to lecture to various educational and community groups on issues concerning women's history, integrating women's studies into the curriculum and on issues concerning Title IX.

The activity which is the subject of this book was supported in whole or in part by the U.S. Office of Education, Department of Education and the St. Louis Park and Robbinsdale Schools. However, the opinions expressed herein do not necessarily reflect the position or policy of the U.S. Office of Education or the School Districts #283 or #281, and no official endorsement by the U.S. Office of Education should be inferred.

Authors' Acknowledgments

The project *Women in World Area Studies* began with the support of two Minneapolis suburban school districts — St. Louis Park and Robbinsdale. The project was funded by the Elementary and Secondary Education Act, Title IV-C for three years. The Northwest Area Foundation funded three additional units on women in Africa, Latin America and Japan.

We would particularly like to thank the following administrators, teachers, editors, consultants and friends who made possible this curriculum unit on *Women in Medieval/Renaissance Europe:*

Michael E. Hickey, Superintendent, and Jim Gavenda of the St. Louis Park Schools.

Professor Kay Reyerson, Department of History, University of Minnesota, who acted as consultant for this unit and who made suggestions for changes in the manuscript.

Nancy Wright who was project assistant and artist for the prototype unit *Women in Medieval/Renaissance Europe.*

Alyce Fuller who provided secretarial skills, suggestions about readability of the text and organized the permissions for the photographs and quoted materials.

Eileen Soderberg who read the text, contributed her typing skills, time and, not incidentally, her safekeeping of the manuscript.

Margo Sprague who donated many of the excellent photographs used in both the book and sound filmstrip.

The University of Minnesota library staff that made possible the research for the series of books of which *Women in Medieval/Renaissance Europe* is a part.

Finally, our husbands, Bert Gross and Thomas Egan, who assisted us by proofreading the manuscript and by understanding the time involved in this curriculum project.